BONES

THE FORENSIC FILES

Bones: The Forensic Files
ISBN: 9781845765903

Published by Titan Books,
A division of Titan Publishing Group Ltd
144 Southwark Street
London
SE1 0UP

First edition October 2009
10 9 8 7 6 5 4 3 2 1

Acknowledgments
The author would like to thank everyone in the cast and crew of *Bones*, the wonderful folks at Twentieth Century Fox, and the amazing crew at Titan Books for contributing your time, memories, and hard work in the creation of this book.

The publishers would also like to thank the cast and crew of *Bones* for all their help with this book. Particular thanks to Hart Hanson for his wonderful introduction. Many thanks also to Debbie Olshan at Twentieth Century Fox.

What did you think of this book? We love to hear from our readers. Please email us at **readerfeedback@titanemail.com** or write to us at the above address.
You can also visit us at **www.titanbooks.com**

To receive advance information, news, competitions, and exclusive Titan offers online, please register as a member by clicking the "sign up" button on our website: **www.titanbooks.com**

A CIP catalogue record for this title is available from the British Library.

Printed and bound in the USA.

BONES

THE FORENSIC FILES

PAUL RUDITIS

CONTENTS

Members of the cast with Hart Hanson and Barry Josephson

INTRODUCTION

BY HART HANSON, EXECUTIVE PRODUCER, BONES

Bones is a pretty solid example of "The Little Engine That Could" variety of TV series. We were not an instant hit. If you were to mathematically diagram our progress—as Brennan and the Squints would no doubt insist upon—the graph you'd see wouldn't be a nice, even, gentle rise in viewership. It'd look more like the EKG print-out of a panic-stricken, moody, agoraphobic, but basically plucky marathon runner being chased by tigers.

But, happily, the overall direction of the graph tends upward. This is what professionals term in series television jargon "very good."

This is because *Bones* has found an extremely loyal audience—or, more precisely, you found us. Bounced around the schedule, pre-empted, displaced by America's Favorite Pastime playoffs and the Gigantic Singing Show, our audience somehow finds us wherever and whenever we land. Our ratings take a resultant hit, temporarily, and then start climbing again. Every time.

"Loyal audience" *sounds* like a condition with only an upside. But it's not. There's a downside.

"*Really?*" you ask.

"*Truly!*" I respond.

Bear with me as I torture the metaphor: if *Bones* is the plucky beleaguered marathon runner mentioned above then the tigers are you, the audience. Yes, I just called you a tiger. And what happens when tigers get messed with? A disturbance, as Siegfried and Roy will tell you. Or one of them will tell you. The other has to write it out on a pad.

As a television series enters the third and fourth seasons with a loyal audience in tow, a crucial dynamic changes. The audience is invested. The show no longer consists of writers, actors, producers, and crew alone... the audience is now part of that equation (as the Squints might put it). In other words, they have a say. And they outnumber those of us toiling on *Bones* here on the Fox Lot in Los Angeles, California.

Our audience of tigers is not only loyal, but noisy. We hear you roaring when you don't like something. We may pursue storylines you don't like or truncate storylines you love; we may anger you, please you, disappoint you, gross you out, or make you laugh at things you find inappropriate; but it is our sincerest hope that you are never bored.

Because it's one thing to be chased by a tiger, maybe even exciting, but it's a disaster to look back and see it yawning.

Having you continue to chase us is the most we can ask. On behalf of the cast and crew of *Bones*, thank you for your interest, your passion, your umbrage, your praise, your indignation, but especially your unwavering loyalty.

And may I say: you look *fantastic* in stripes.

THE KNEE BONE'S CONNECTED TO THE THIGH BONE...

INTO SEASON THREE

Call it a "Crimedy."
Part forensic mystery, part romantic comedy, Bones has managed something very few television shows can accomplish in this day of multiple channels providing a wide range of viewing choices. On average, most new network shows fail to make their mark from the start, or they premiere to big ratings that either hold steady or slowly drop over time. While Bones launched with a respectable audience, it has managed to grow, both in popularity and critical acclaim, with every passing season, whilst being bounced all over the Fox schedule. "It feels so good," admits executive producer Barry Josephson, "because the show, no matter where it airs, has taken its audience with it. And that's the most satisfying thing."

"There have been a few shows that take off in their second year, but very few that take off in their third," notes executive producer Hart Hanson. "Each season we do better. Someone always asks me why that happens and I don't know. But I like it."

This unusual path to success may be understandable—if not entirely fitting—for a series like Bones. As executive producer Stephen Nathan explains, "I think to a certain extent it was because we were an odd kind of show. I think people thought it was a serious procedural when it started and it was always this kind of odd amalgam of romantic comedy and procedural. I think it had far more of an eccentric feel than people actually assumed. So it took them a little bit longer to find the show and when they did, I think they started telling their friends."

Going into the third season of this unique show, much of the groundwork had already been laid for the story the writers were telling. F.B.I. Special Agent Seeley Booth and forensic anthropologist Dr. Temperance Brennan are teamed up to solve crimes using advanced scientific methods combined with tried and true investigative skills, while ignoring the romantic tension simmering between them. Working out of the Jeffersonian Institute with a staff of "Squints," they tackle some of the most challenging federal murder cases. But it isn't the murders that keep bringing viewers back and the producers know it.

"The main story engine of the series is the Booth and Brennan relationship," explains Hanson. "I don't mean the cases. So far we don't seem to be in any danger of running out of cases. People keep murdering people out

Sweets: Are you normally this protective of him, Dr. Brennan?

Brennan: We're partners. Our lives depend on being protective of each other.

Sweets: And you feel the same way, Agent Booth?

Booth: Sweets, I can only hope that one day you know what a real partnership is.

in the real world and giving us ideas." Hanson is referring to his two lead characters, individuals that would seem to be totally opposite in every way possible, but are really more alike than they are ready to admit. Over the years Brennan and Booth have taken their differing approaches to life and used their viewpoints to learn from one another and to grow, both individually and as a pair. And everyone around them—and the audience at home—is just waiting for them to get together.

When last we met our heroes, Booth and Brennan—or "Bones" as he calls her—were left standing at the altar. Just not *their* altar. They were members of the wedding party of Dr. Jack Hodgins and Angela Montenegro, which was unexpectedly postponed due to a previous marital commitment on the part of the bride. Recent graduate, Dr. Zack Addy, had gone off to Iraq to undertake the important job of identifying the dead. And the newest member of the team, Dr. Camille

Saroyan, was still getting accustomed to being in charge of a group of distinctly individual personalities.

Going into season three, the writers would maintain the delicate balance of bringing Booth and Brennan closer together while keeping them enough apart to whet the audience's appetite. They would start a search for Angela's missing husband, bring Zack home, and introduce a new character in the role of Dr. Lance Sweets as played by John Francis Daley. But the biggest obstacle in the story the writers would face came from off-screen in the form of the writers' strike. "Probably many of our problems in season three came from the decision we made to advance as though the strike was not going to happen," Hart Hanson admits. "Then it got to the point where, 'Oh my god, it certainly could happen. This could actually happen.'"*Bones*, a traditionally episodic series with self-contained mysteries every episode, made a notable shift in

storytelling for the third season. At the network's suggestion, the writers came up with a serial killer storyline that was to be told over multiple episodes in a season-long arc. An intricate mystery was laid out that would affect each of the characters and change the makeup of the cast by season's end. It was a massive undertaking that was thrown in disarray when the traditional number of episodes was cut from twenty-two to fifteen.

"No one knew how long the strike was going to last," Stephen Nathan recalls. "So no one knew how many episodes we had to make that arc graceful. It was just a patchwork toward the end of the year to get us back on track. I think we did it, but it was very, very difficult." Part of that difficulty came from the fact that season three did not end with the writers' strike; several episodes were aired afterwards as well.

The writers ended their twelve pre-strike episodes on a cliffhanger that would allow them to pick up the following season if that was all they filmed. During a night out with the gang in 'The Wannabe in the Weeds,' Booth was shot while protecting Brennan from his newly acquired stalker. Fade to black. End season. But the season didn't go out that way. The network held a handful of episodes that were produced before the strike to air late in the spring, including that fateful episode. Then they requested two additional episodes. One of those episodes had to bring Booth back from his near death experience and wrap up Brennan's family drama. The other story had to bring closure to the mystery of the Gormogon serial killer.

"We had to deal with Gormogon and Zack all in one episode instead of through the back third," Hanson explains. "That was episode fifteen. Generally you would

have had another seven episodes to play that story out—and we were going to play out that story. We were going to meet Booth's family in that episode; meet his grandfather. And that all just went into the crapper because of the foreshortened strike season. There are no excuses in television, but that's why I think a good chunk of our audience was dissatisfied with the Zack story. We did our best to fold it in and make it work and apparently it wasn't as successful as we thought it would be."

Regrets aside, the writers did leave an opening for Zack to return in season four so they could help flesh out his story a little further. They also used the rest of season three to present new challenges in the work and personal lives of all their characters. The audience learned more about Brennan's family, Booth's teenage self, Angela and Hodgins' quirky relationship, Cam's reliance on flesh over bones. But most importantly, and frustratingly, the audience was given a tease into the possibility of a romance between Brennan and Booth with a kiss under the mistletoe.

SEASON THREE

David Boreanaz: *Special Agent Seeley Booth*

Emily Deschanel: *Dr. Temperance Brennan*

Michaela Conlin: *Angela Montenegro*

Eric Millegan: *Dr. Zach Addy*

Tamara Taylor: *Dr. Camille Saroyan*

TJ Thyne: *Dr. Jack Hodgins*

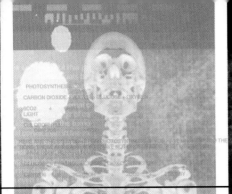

THE WIDOW'S SON IN THE WINDSHIELD

WRITTEN BY HART HANSON   **DIRECTED BY** IAN TOYNTON

GUEST STARRING: PATRICIA BELCHER (CAROLINE JULIAN), RAPHAEL SBARGE (DOUG DOYLEY), EUGENE BYRD (CLARK EDISON), CYNTHIA PRESTON (AMELIA TRATTNER), ANDREW JAMES ALLEN (JASON HARKNESS), SUZANNE FORD (RONA SUMNER), MICHAEL CANAVAN (LEO SUMNER), DWAYNE MACOPSON (D.C. BEAT COP), J. SKYLAR TESTA (SK8R DRIVER)

- A human skull fell from a freeway overpass and crashed through the windshield of a car. The skull is completely devoid of flesh and has scoring in an **ungual pattern**. Evidence of scalloped and denticulated mastication indicates that a human gnawed on the skull.
- An enlarged **osteoma** in the skull matches an X-ray obtained from an ear nose and throat specialist. The victim is identified as violin prodigy Gavin Nichols.
- Microscopic grit in the skull is determined to be a rare pink syenite that was used in the construction of a local deserted bank.
- A collection of artifacts is found in the sealed vault inside the bank along with a silver skeleton set in a ritualistic pose. Some of the skeleton parts have been replaced by real bone from six different victims, that also show teeth marks.
- A mark in the scoring indicates that the cannibal has a diamond insert in his right canine. The evidence leads to a young man named Jason Harkness who confesses to the crime.
- The older bones show evidence of being chewed on by a second person, indicating that another suspect had brought Harkness in on his work. Before Harkness can be questioned, he is found dead in his cell.

Zack's premature return from Iraq was only one part of an overall experience that Eric Millegan believes had a profound effect on his character. "It shook [Zack's] confidence a bit," he explains. "It was kind of twofold. On one hand he was out there on his own, not working for Dr. Brennan, so that was giving him confidence. But I think when he got sent home early, it kind of rocked his perception of who he is."

This episode also marks the team's first encounter with the Gormogon serial killer. The Gormogon idea came as a bit of a surprise considering the show's executive producers had been on record for not feeling the love for those kinds of plotlines. Creator Hart Hanson explains, "I'm not a big fan of serial killer stories. The bad guy in a serial killer plot is usually crazy; he's usually nuts. I don't find clinically insane characters very interesting. They're just evil and they do it because the

dog told them to or whatever. I have a slight bias against it. But I am surrounded by very intelligent people who are not so hide-bound."

The network convinced the writer/producers to create a serial killer for the show. Once that was done, it was just a matter of how to make it work for *Bones*.

The answer came out of another idea that Fox was interested in pursuing. "They wanted us to be open to the idea of a possible video game or online component of the serial killer storyline that could be interactive," Hanson explains. "The first thing that popped into my mind was that we would find the Gormogon's lair and it would be really interesting and full of things to click on and leave clues. So I kind of worked backwards from there."

This led to the idea of a killer who was fighting against the influence of secret societies. Hanson goes on, "Because

Booth: Caroline, am I any more annoying than I used to be?

Caroline: I find that you maintain an impressively consistent level of annoyance at all times, why?

Booth: Nothing. Reality check.

Hodgins is a secret society guy, I liked the idea of a serial killer who was acting to stop the pernicious influence of secret societies in the world. It resonated for us. So that's when it started coming together."

Executive producer Stephen Nathan adds, "We wanted to play with that element of craziness as much as we could and make it as arcane, mysterious and bizarre as we could, and therefore try to impose a certain rationality on the insanity. We created this whole mythology that had existed for many, many years and had a strong logical component to it, so that we could get one of our own involved."

Their serial killer became a member of the Gormogon Society, which, at its core, was opposed to the actions of the Freemason Society. The killer targeted members of that society, and used their bones in the creation of a horrific skeleton.

Hart Hanson recalls that the silver skeleton came from the answer to a simple question. "We're the bones show, so what's something horrific we can do with a serial killer in bones? It became that the serial killer was recreating the skeleton of a perfect human being, finding members of secret societies who were monstrously successful in their chosen field and taking a bone—like the violinist's finger. That's how we got to the Gormogon."

Not that they stopped there. Hanson admits that they maybe went a little too far with their serial killer. "Alas, alack, it's just how things work," he notes. "Because we needed a good solid episode and a good beginning, we had the cannibal stuff. Then you're stuck with it. It sounded like a good idea for the episode and now the guy has to be a cannibal as well. It was set and we had to go forward with the serial killer."

Ungual pattern: A configuration that is uniform in spacing but not in depth as if caused by a hoof, nail, or claw.

Osteoma: A type of bone spur that typically grows from the skull down into the sinus cavity. Can cause headaches or infected sinuses.

'See the World' by Gomez, *See the World*

THE SOCCER MOM IN THE MINI-VAN

WRITTEN BY ELIZABETH BENJAMIN   DIRECTED BY ALLAN KROEKER

SPECIAL GUEST STAR: RYAN O'NEAL (MAX KEENAN)
GUEST STARRING: PATRICIA BELCHER (CAROLINE JULIAN), DEBORAH ZOE (SPECIAL AGENT KATHERINE FROST), ERICH ANDERSON (JEREMY NASH), SCOUT TAYLOR-COMPTON (CELIA NASH), RICHARD COX (LEONARD HUNTZINGER), CHRIS TARDIO (DANNY VALENTI), RON CANADA (SPECIAL AGENT SAM REILLY)

- A female victim is found in the charred remains of a van registered to a Jeremy Nash. Nash identifies the victim as his wife, Amy.
- **Triphenylmethane dye** and **iron sulfate** are imbedded in the manubrium and the flesh of the victim, suggesting a home-made tattoo. Angela reconstructs the image to reveal a symbol of the National Liberation Army.
- Amy Nash's true identity is determined to be June Harris, who disappeared after being named a suspect in the murder of a police officer in the 1970s. Caroline Julian reveals that she recently made a deal with the victim to turn herself in.
- Watch remnants found in the explosive debris match the watch Harris's partner, Neal Watkins, used to create his bombs.
- A superficial gunshot wound in the victim's shoulder produces a bullet that matches the gun used to kill the police officer thirty years earlier. Microscopic lead particles on the **metacarpals** of the left hand reveal a bullet path that suggests June Harris was attempting to protect the officer from Watkins when she was shot.
- Neal Watkins is also found shot dead in a murder that was staged as a suicide.
- The bomber left a thumbprint on the watch, identifying the killer as Jeremy Nash. He also killed his wife, thinking that she had never stopped loving Watkins. In reality she had just been meeting with Watkins to convince him to turn himself in.

At Booth's request, Caroline Julian arranges for Brennan to have a private visitation with her father. Brennan is initially reluctant to go, but she relents and the pair have an awkward reunion. Max apologizes for disappointing his daughter, but Brennan fears that he has only apologized because he wants her to testify on his behalf. Seeing parallels with her own life in her current case, Brennan later attempts to make amends with her father.

One of the major contributing factors to the development of the Temperance Brennan character is found in her ways of dealing with her fractured family situation. Abandoned by her parents and her brother when she was a teen, Brennan grew up in the foster system. In recent years, she has been reunited with her brother and her father, and discovered that her mother died as a result of a complicated past that somewhat mirrored the case of Amy Nash/June Harris. With her rogue of a father back in her life, Brennan is

Brennan: ...My father is a criminal.

Max: An outlaw. There's a difference.

*Brennan: Subtle distinctions like that are lost on me and,
I imagine, your victims.*

learning to accept that life is a bit more ambiguous than her science would have her believe.

"She's beginning to understand how contradictory life and emotions can be," notes Emily Deschanel. "She can now understand some of the motives her father had for doing some of the bad things he's done. Brennan never would have been able to see that at the beginning of the series. She's grown in that way. I think it's always positive when someone can learn from a relationship or an experience. Brennan certainly learns from her relationship with her family, particularly her father."

While the case teams Booth up with his mentor, who may also be a suspect, Hodgins is partnered with the attractive Special Agent Frost from the F.B.I. bomb unit. The two share many bizarre interests and their close working relationship leaves Hodgins stammering whenever she's around, but Angela is not concerned. She knows, without a doubt, that he will remain true to her.

Triphenylmethane dye: A family of synthetic organic dyes found in ballpoint ink.

Iron sulfate: A chemical compound used as a pigment.

Metacarpal: A bone in the hands and feet, located between the carpus and phalanges.

'Perfect Day' by Lou Reed, *Perfect Day*

DEATH IN THE SADDLE

WRITTEN BY *JOSH BERMAN*   DIRECTED BY *CRAIG ROSS JR.*

- A body is found in the Virginia woods with a fatal stab wound to the frontal bone. The victim's hands were tied and his feet were severed and buried. Absence of pronounced **ecchymosis** on the wrists and the lack of **hemorrhagic tissue** on the feet prove that he was bound and his feet were cut off post mortem. Based on the victim's fingerprints he is identified as Ed Milner.
- An emollient around the nose and mouth is determined to be sunscreen formulated for horses, while the contents of the victim's stomach are consistent with a horse's diet. Research reveals that the condition of the body also matches rituals associated with horses.
- The victim's last credit card purchase leads investigators to a retreat specializing in a "Pony Play Fantasy" fetish. In an interview the victim's fetish partner, Annie Oakley, the woman confirms that Milner's wife recently found out about their horseplay.
- The shape of the wound to the forehead suggests a hoof knife was the murder weapon. The same knife was used to sever the feet and tiny nicks in the bone around the eyeballs indicate that the murderer also gauged out the eyes. All evidence indicates that the killer was skilled with a knife. Dr. Anne Marie Ostenback (Annie Oakley) admits to killing the victim because he was planning to end their fantasy play and return to his wife.

When Cam brings Brennan in on a case that concerns human remains that are more flesh than bone, Brennan suspects that it is a ploy to ease her and Booth back into their partnership. Brennan refuses to acknowledge that Booth not talking Zack out of going to Iraq put a strain on their relationship. It seems she's speaking the truth when the case, which covers a range of topics from a pony-play fetish to vegetarianism, sees the pair easily slipping back into their usual banter.

"That is the great key to *Bones*," states Hart Hanson, referring to the story "arenas" he likes to put his characters in, where Booth and Brennan debate on a variety of subjects. "When we see the world through the lenses that Booth and

Brennan see the world, that's where the power of the series resides. She is very rational, very empirical: she believes in measurement and believing in what you can see. And he is more about emotion, and a spiritual and humanist approach to the world. Everything has to be siphoned through that. The tension between them stems from the way they view the world, as does the comedy between them. It's what creates the sexual tension as well. How could people with such differing views of the universe ever get together? The more we do that, the more believable it is that they don't simply fall into bed every episode."

Exploring these subcultures allows the writers to delve deeper into their characters' thoughts and motivations. It also gives the production staff a chance to broaden their own horizons by creating these unique worlds for the show. Sometimes, the dictates of these worlds present a challenge for the staff, while other times it's easier than one might think. "We had a lot of the pony-play props made by someone who supplies that type of gear to 'enthusiasts' all over the world," recalls prop master Ian Scheibel. "The rest was found either at a pet store or a tack shop."

Booth: What was with all the lying? "We've got voice tapes and a public display of sexual paraphernalia?"

Brennan: I was role playing. I was being all lard ass and good cop.

Booth: Hard ass and bad cop, Bones. Hard ass and bad cop.

Angela also explores an alternative belief when she agrees to undergo hypnosis to recall the name of her forgotten husband. She's skeptical of the procedure, but the experience eventually leads her to a book that she was reading in Fiji that has a wedding photo she used as a bookmark. The image of her husband is not clear, but it does have the name "Grayson" on the back, which jogs her memory of his full name: Grayson Barasa.

"You'd think she would just jump right in," Michaela Conlin says, recalling her initial surprise over the skepticism her normally unconventional character felt toward hypnosis. "I'm waiting for the day when I, Michaela, have something to be hypnotized for. I think it would be kind of hilarious. I went to a psychic last summer. I'm into that stuff. I mean, why not? Life is hard enough. It might be good to have a little help in that department. But I thought it was really interesting that Angela was almost conservative about it. She was very hesitant, much more so than I thought she would be. I think that in some respects she knew that this crazy life she was leading was going to come up."

Ecchymosis: An injury to biological tissue, i.e. a bruise or contusion.
Hemorrhagic tissue: Tissue that shows evidence of ruptured blood vessels or any escape of blood.

THE SECRET IN THE SOIL

WRITTEN BY *KARINE ROSENTHAL*   **DIRECTED BY** *STEPHEN DEPAUL*

GUEST STARRING: JOHN FRANCIS DALEY (DR. LANCE SWEETS), ERIN CHAMBERS (KAT), ROBERT BLESSE (CHARLIE ROGAN), BETH GRANT (LIZBETH HARDING), SCOOT MCNAIRY (NOEL LIFTIN), GILL GAYLE (GAVIN LEE), DENISE CROSBY (MARGIE CURTIS), CHRISTOPHER DARGA (ANDREW HARDING), CAMERON WATSON (LYNDON PAGE)

- The body of a middle-aged male is found with an internal temperature of 127 degrees, suggesting the body was cooked before it was dumped. The victim is identified as Franklin Curtis.
- A button pattern on the remaining skin tissue suggests that the victim was pressed up against another body during the heating process.
- The presence of an agricultural pest found on pineapple plants leads the investigation to a local composting facility. Considering that a large compost heap can reach temperatures of 170 degrees, it is seen as the likely murder spot.
- Bruising and fresh hairline fractures on the femurs are consistent with defensive wounds. A hole in the sternum is determined to be a **sternal foramen**.
- A female victim's remains are found in the compost heap. Multiple broken ribs and a severely fractured sternum are consistent with inexpert use of CPR.
- The second victim, Emma, also has a sternal foramen like the primary victim. A DNA test confirms Emma was Curtis's illegitimate daughter.
- DNA similar to the first victim is found under Emma's fingernails, revealing the murderer was Curtis's other daughter, Kat. She had fought with Emma, thinking the young woman was another of her father's mistresses. Curtis later died in a fight with Kat's friend, Charlie, who had helped hide Emma's body.

Booth and Brennan work on trust exercises with their new and rather young therapist, Dr. Lance Sweets. Booth's superiors at the F.B.I. are considering dissolving his partnership with Brennan in the wake of him arresting her father. Dr. Sweets has been assigned as the final arbiter in the decision. Sweets administers a personality test to assist him in his analysis and to give Booth and Brennan a chance to examine their relationship.

The addition of Dr. Sweets to the cast grew out of Booth's sessions with Dr. Gordon Wyatt in the prior season. The original plan was to have Stephen Fry continue the role of the kindly though somewhat intimidating therapist, integrating him into the series beyond his work with Booth. "We worked up a bunch of stories where he would have been very useful to us," Hart Hanson recalls. "And it just opened up the cases to have that guy." The plan, however, did not come to pass. Hanson explains, "Unfortunately, Stephen Fry is the busiest man in the world and could not possibly commit to that. By that time we had realized that [the therapist] would be a great character for the show. It could open things up in the world as much as Cam had opened things up in the lab when we brought her in to be the coroner. We thought that this extra person in our band of merry crime solvers would be a great thing."

When the writers initially conceived of Gordon Wyatt back in season two, they were looking for a "huge figure" that Booth couldn't intimidate physically or mentally. But when it came time to cast someone else in the role of therapist, as well as forensic psychologist and profiler, they had to move in a different direction. "You can't go, 'Oh, let's get another great big, smart guy.'" Hanson explains. "The world of the series has to be more interesting than that. Just like you wouldn't go find another tall, pale, willowy

Booth: ...Come on it's the weekend. Abandoned building, surrounded by acres of secluded land... use your imagination. Teenagers. Hormones.

Brennan: You're saying they're here to fornicate.

Booth: Nice image. Very biblical.

guy to play an intern after Zack was gone. You'd want to replace him with something different that opened up another door." Hanson was a fan of John Francis Daley since his work on the cult hit TV series *Freaks and Geeks*. He rediscovered the young talent while watching a writer friend's series, *Kitchen Confidential*, and quickly snapped the actor up for his show.

"It couldn't have gone easier," John Francis Daley says of his being accepted into the cast. "Everyone there was so welcoming and easy to work with. It was like being adopted into this family that already existed and very quickly becoming part of it. Every cast member is really nice

and they all have their own sort of chemistry, which makes it always interesting to do scenes with them and just hang out with them on the set."

Not that Daley's character had as easy a time being accepted into the group. "To start off with they didn't really trust Sweets. They didn't know all of his intentions. To them he was just the person that had to say whether or not they were fit to continue working together after Brennan's dad was arrested. I think, very quickly, Sweets became aware of their chemistry and took a personal interest in this dynamic between the two of them."

Sternal foramen: A congenital abnormality found in the lower third section of the sternum.

'Bones' by 8mm, *Songs to Love and Die by...*
'You' by Fisher, *The Lovely Years*

MUMMY IN THE MAZE

WRITTEN BY *SCOTT WILLIAMS*   **DIRECTED BY** *MARITA GRABIAK*

GUEST STARRING: RIDER STRONG (GREGG LISCOMBE), AZURA SKYE (AMBER KIPLER), NATHAN ANDERSON (EMT PETE GELLER), VINCE GRANT (PASTOR BILL JONAS), TERRY RHOADS (DR. POTOSKA), JUDY PRESCOTT (MARGIE SHAW), PAUL CASSELL (DON SHAW), LYNSEY BARTILSON (SISTER), LAURENCE COHEN (DAN JAUSER), CAKER FOLLEY (LOLA)

• The mummified corpse of a girl that has been dead for a year is found in a Halloween maze. A married couple believes the remains to be their daughter, Megan Shaw, but she has only been missing one week.

• A second mummified body is later found at Shoreline Amusement Park—where Megan disappeared.

• A sketch of the first victim is matched to Stella Higgins, a teen that disappeared from the Shoreline Amusement Park a year earlier. The second victim is identified as Judith Suzanne Evans who went missing from the park two years earlier. Stress fractures in both of Evans's tibias, tears to the **medial collateral** and **anterior cruciate ligaments** in both knees, and compressions to vertebrae C1 through C7 suggest that she, like Higgins, was buried alive.

• Toxicology results on both girls reveal heavy stimulants in their systems that would cause heart rates to accelerate dangerously. That combined with evidence of hundreds of tarantula bites on Higgins leads investigators to believe the girls were literally scared to death.

• Lacquer on the bodies was infused with particulates common to machine shops and a spore found in a Hawaiian orchid hybrid. Investigators determine that Megan Shaw is still alive and being held at a flower shop near subway tracks. There, the killer is revealed to be the EMT who treated all three girls after a pair of park employees had attacked them.

It's almost fitting that a story that begins in a children's Halloween hay maze should end in the darkened labyrinth of tunnels beneath the subway. Location manager Deborah Laub counts the Southern California Edison Eagle Rock Substation as one of her favorite locations in the series. "It's an old 1920s electrical substation," Laub says. "Each room is spooky and other worldly and the entire building looks great on film. We shot here for the pedestrian underpass, subway access shaft, various subway sections and the snake room."

Above ground, Angela's husband, Grayson Barasa, is found. In spite of the investigator's attempts to woo Angela back to her hunky husband, she reaffirms her love for Hodgins and they join their friends for some Halloween festivities.

"When I was first told we were going to do Cher," Michaela Conlin recalls, "I thought it was going to be TJ and me as Sonny and Cher. But then I heard it was going to be the Bob Mackey thing with the headdress and I was like, 'Wasn't that the dress where there's no midsection?' Luckily all the ladies were sort of scantily clad, so we could all quickly put our robes on together when they yelled, 'Cut.'"

It turns out that Conlin herself was, unknowingly, the one responsible for planting the Cher idea in Hart Hanson's head. She once performed a spot-on impression of the famed actress/singer for him, and so when it came time to dole out the Halloween costumes for the characters, Hanson felt it would be a natural fit. One down, that left five other diverse characters to outfit.

Hanson relates how Emily Deschanel reacted when he told her that he was thinking of Brennan as Wonder Woman. "She just gasped like a two year-old girl and said, 'I have always loved Wonder Woman. I have a costume from when I was a kid!'" Deschanel confirms her love of the Amazonian character. "She was my childhood idol," she enthuses. "So powerful. It was a dream come true. I actually was Wonder Woman for Halloween a few years ago." Though, she admits, "After a day in that costume, I was over it. It's uncomfortable to essentially wear a corset and underwear all day long. I felt pretty exposed, but it was worth it."

Booth's costume would prove more of a challenge, due to David Boreanaz's mischievous desire to get into the

Brennan: Who is stronger? Catwoman or Wonder Woman?

Hodgins & Zack (in unison): Wonder Woman.

Brennan: I concur. Vehemently.

Halloween spirit. "All David's ideas were self-deprecating," Hanson says. "He wanted to be in a fat suit or cover his face completely. And I said, 'David, I'm sorry, but this is a network show, whatever you are, you have to be kind of hot.' And then it popped into my head that if he were imitating a nerd—one of the Squints—he'd get what he wanted and I'd get what I wanted. He was basically Clark Kent."

Hanson recalls his initial intention for Cam was to make her a woman of the old West. "Then I went, 'What the hell? You just told David he has to look hot. Here's one of the most beautiful women in the world and you're going to put her in a hoop dress? I don't think so. Catwoman!'" Tamara Taylor was delighted, "What brown girl doesn't want to be Catwoman?" she says. "I mean, Eartha Kitt! I'm also a bit of a comic book geek, so I was over the moon." Taylor adds, grinning, "I think my husband enjoyed it more than I did."

The producers also had fun making Zack the business end of a cow and putting Hodgins in, as Hanson puts it, "One of those crazy costumes where you always have to tell people who you are." Which is how Hodgins became Edward J. Smith, captain of the doomed ship Titanic, and the cast got to let down their collective hair and have some fun.

Medial collateral ligament (MCL): One of the four major ligaments in the knee, the MCL is composed of strong fibrous material that control excessive motion to the knee joint.

Anterior cruciate ligament (ACL): Another of the four major ligaments in the knee, it attaches to the femur at the back of the joint and passes down through the knee joint to the tibia.

'Monster' by The Automatic, *Not Accepted Anywhere*

'Young Men Dead' by The Black Angels, *Passover*

'Still Alright' by Adam Merrin, *Have One*

INTERN IN THE INCINERATOR

WRITTEN BY CHRISTOPHER AMBROSE   *DIRECTED BY* JEFF WOOLNOUGH

GUEST STARRING: XANDER BERKELEY (DR. BANCROFT), TERRELL TILFORD (DR. KYLE ALDRIDGE), SCOTT ALLEN RINKER (DR. EVAN KLIMKEW), TOM VIRTUE (DR. TED REARDON), ROCHELLE AYTES (FELICIA SAROYAN), SAM JONES III (TYLER NEVILLE)

- A charred human skeleton is found in the Jeffersonian incinerator. The level of charring suggests the body had been dead for six to eight hours. Angela identifies the victim as intern Kirsten Reardon.
- Zack and Hodgins experiment with a fabricated body to determine that the victim fell from the top floor of the building. Puncturing of the aorta and left lung indicate she was stabbed to death first.
- Outgoing calls from the victim's cell phone are matched to a number belonging to the head of the Jeffersonian's Middle East department, Dr. Aldridge.
- The positioning of the victim's wound suggests a single point of entry through the back, leading investigators to believe that Reardon fell on a sharp object. A copper fragment is retrieved from the fifth rib, but nothing in the inventory matches the artifact.
- The body of Dr. Aldridge is found hanging in the Gormogon vault after an apparent suicide. However, it is determined that he was poisoned with the drug **Succinylcholine**.
- Records show the artifact that Reardon fell on was shipped to a P.O. Box in Arlington. The head of the Authentications department, Dr. Klimkew, is found to be smuggling Iraqi artifacts and committed the murders to cover his crime.

A charred body in the Jeffersonian incinerator brings this crime a little closer to home, especially when it's discovered that Angela knew the victim. It is also a perfect example of how the production team takes the most gruesome murders and gives them an almost comedic spin. In this case, the audience gets a look at the Squints from the perspective of the blue-collar workers who discover the first body. "The whole incinerator scene at the beginning with the two guys discovering that charred body was a real riot," first assistant director Kent Genzlinger recalls. "[Director] Jeff Woolnough brought a lot of humor to it, and still brought us a grizzly, toasty body at the same time."

The charred body is also an example of the kind of coordination required between departments to create a prop body that can be exposed to flame without burning. "That's definitely a three-part conversation," Genzlinger explains. "We do a lot of pre-planning with Chris Yagher in makeup effects and Randy Torpin, who does our physical effects. We figure out what the body can stand and what it can't stand. We have a body that's burned and a body that isn't, and cut between them so that we can really use the flames on the burned body and maybe put the flames in the foreground for the body that we can't burn too much. We also threw in some visual effects that Derek Bird at Look Effects did, in order to make all three parts go from different levels of burning."

But the coordination does not stop there, as Genzlinger explains, "And of course

Zack: We're calling him Gormogon now.

Hodgins: Excellent name. And historically accurate.

then we're working a lot with Fox Safety in order to vent the stage, make sure there's nothing toxic and flammable in the way. That worked out really well. The rig that Randy built for the incinerator and the way the body worked for Chris, you definitely got a little crispy critter in there."

Considering the victim was authenticating items from the cannibalistic serial killer's vault, the writers were able to bring in the season's overall arc as the Squints begin to suspect that the murder is related to the sociopath. It's easier for them to think in those terms than to accept that the murderer may be one of "their own."

Furthering the balance of humor with the macabre, a subplot has Cam asking Booth to be her date to her dad's sixtieth birthday party, since she never told her family that they split up. Although he's uncomfortable with the arrangement, it doesn't really become an issue until Cam's sister kisses Booth. It's a secret that Booth thinks will only bring more friction to the fighting sisters, but it oddly helps them grow a little closer. "I thought the actress that played my sister was fantastic," Tamara Taylor says in regards to the episode that taught her more about her own character. "The scenes between my sister, Booth and myself were really, really fun to play. I didn't know until it was written that that was the dynamic that Cam had with her sister. Those things create these different levels to Cam that I'm enjoying playing."

Succinylcholine: Muscle relaxant that in high doses can stop heart and lung function.

THE BOY IN THE TIME CAPSULE

WRITTEN BY *JANET LIN*   DIRECTED BY *CHAD LOWE*

GUEST STARRING: JOHN FRANCIS DALEY (DR. LANCE SWEETS), PATRICK FISCHLER (GIL BATES), PATRICK FABIAN (TERRY STINSON), KRISTIN BAUER (JANELLE STINSON), RAY BAKER (DANIEL DILLON), RICK RAVANELLO (JOHN ADAMSON), STEPHON FULLER (DARWIN BANKS)

- A high school time capsule from the 1980s is opened to reveal the organic remains of a classmate. A sketch of the skull found in the sludge matches the yearbook picture of Roger Dillon. The victim has a fracture on the right clavicle and indications of a grade 2 **acromioclavicular joint** separation suggesting his arm was forcefully twisted behind his back.
- Traces of a common pesticide are found with the body. The pesticide was used in a housing development at the time, where a cheerleader named Janelle Stinson lived. A comparison of Dillon's image with a photo of Stinson's son leads investigators to believe that the boy is the victim's son.
- A floppy disk not listed in the contents of the capsule is found. It contains a computer game model that would have been considerably advanced for 1987. Dillon's best friend, Gil Bates, explains that they had been partners, raising money through odd jobs to develop the game.
- It appears that the weapon was thrust into the victim's neck, severing the carotid artery and jugular vein. A stain on the mandible is liquid petroleum with microscopic particles of granite, suggesting the weapon was an asphalt shovel.
- Bates worked paving driveways as a teen and had access to an asphalt shovel. He admits that the accidental death was the result of a fight because the victim told him that he wanted to give the money earmarked for their game to a girl.

The high school setting that surrounds this crime reminds Booth of his years as a teen sports hero, much to the chagrin of Bones and the Squints who realize that their friend was "that guy" in school. "Golden Boy" Booth presses Brennan to share some of her past with him, and he winds up laughing at her when she tells him an embarrassing story. When the subject comes up at their counseling session, Sweets suggests that Booth should share an equally private story, but all Booth can come up with are tales that brag about his accomplishments. Eventually, he shares a personal story that doesn't present him in the best light, and

Brennan reassures him that he is no longer "that guy." Booth apologizes to her by way of a gift to help her get over her past humiliation.

The nostalgia element of this episode spurred the characters to talk about themselves during their high school days, but what about the actors who play them? Some of the audience first met John Francis Daley as a teen when he starred in the short-lived but critically acclaimed series, *Freaks and Geeks* (coincidentally, also set in the eighties). The rest of the cast, however, spent their teenage years living far more typical lives as they explain who *they* were in high school...

Emily Deschanel: "I was pretty much a nerd/dork. I was into theater and acting. In junior high I was ridiculed. High school got a bit better, but by no stretch of the imagination could you call me popular. I would spend my lunch break in the physics classroom, going over my lab notebook, if that gives you any idea. I guess Brennan and I weren't all that different."

Michaela Conlin: "I was really, really busy. I'm from Pennsylvania and I had a big dream to go to New York. I really wanted to leave Allentown, PA and go to New York. I was president of the drama club. I was vice president of my class. I was very busy in high school. It wasn't too dire. I had a good time."

TJ Thyne: "My friends would tell you I'm still the exact same guy: Loves acting, loves sports, loves learning, loves his family, loves his friends, loves laughing and making people laugh. Someone that enjoys life fully and challenges himself constantly to make it better for himself and for others. Because, hell, ain't life grand! I mean it really, really is!"

Tamara Taylor: "I didn't hang with any particular group of people. My interests were so diverse. I didn't even go to high school prom. I was just kind of the punky girl that sat in the corner reading her book. A little bit of a loner."

Eric Millegan: "I was very, very involved. I was in the musicals. I was in every club. I was in student council. I was valedictorian. I had skipped the seventh grade, so I was younger than everybody in my class. I looked young for my age anyway. I look back at pictures in high school and I'm like, 'Oh my god, I look like an elementary school student.' I was like the kid among the kids."

Acromioclavicular joint: The AC joint is located at the top of the shoulder between the acromion and the clavicle.

'Bandstand in the Sky' by Pete Yorn, *Nightcrawler*

From a production standpoint, the eighties nostalgia element was a very specific challenge for the prop department. They were charged with obtaining vintage items to both set the scene and to appear out of the time capsule. Finding objects for the time capsule was complicated by the fact that every item had to emerge from a gooey sludge. "There is always a lot of planning involved when a prop has to go from dirty to clean," prop master Ian Scheibel reveals. "As soon as you put a paper prop—like an album cover, high school yearbook, or photograph—into wet sludge it starts deteriorating. Also, you have to understand that a script does not get shot in chronological order. Sometimes props have to go through several stages or looks but we might shoot those stages in reverse order. We might shoot the scene where the Guns N' Roses album has sludge all over it and then, ten minutes later, we shoot it dry and relatively clean."

It all begins, naturally, with a thorough reading of the script. Scheibel creates his prop list based on the items specifically mentioned by name, as well as choices made from research to add the kind of items that might also be included but were not called out by the writers. "From that point, there are a lot of decisions based on availability and legal issues," he adds lightly. "Hard to believe, but there are those copyright-holders out there that would prefer that no one saw their product coming out of a mass of liquefied flesh."

Scheibel admits to spending an enormous amount of time online, both researching the props and buying them. For this episode he received over 400 emails from Ebay alone responding to requests for props. "That may have been the most challenging episode of the season," he admits. "That's why I get two or three or more of many of the props. All I can say is thank god for the internet and a great team in the department."

Every episode has its own challenges, but this particular one presented the prop team with seven days to come up with three of each item on the prop master's list of vintage stash. In the end, they gathered the following mementoes for the time capsule:

Angela: I was all about Barbie.

Hodgins: She was my first anatomy lesson. I was confused for years.

Cam: What about Ken? I felt so sorry for him.

- *Appetite For Destruction* by Guns N' Roses
- *The Wishing Chair* by 10,000 Maniacs
- Pee-wee Herman talking doll
- Mr. T lunchbox
- William Perry bobblehead doll
- *Life* magazines with Warren Beatty and Dustin Hoffman on the cover
- Hands Across America t-shirts
- Rubik's Cube
- Simon Game
- Punky Brewster poster
- Michael Jordan's #23 jersey
- Air Jordan tennis shoes circa 1987
- *St. Elmo's Fire* on Beta tape
- *Pet Cemetery* by Stephen King
- *Flowers in the Attic* by Virginia Andrews
- Custom pocket watch
- School mascot doll
- Football helmet
- Recreations of the *New York Times* and period teen magazines.

Determining Time of Death

The ability to pinpoint the exact time a victim died is integral in the investigation of a murder. The more specific forensics investigators can be in honing in on the time of death the more instrumental it can be in finding a killer, especially if the suspect does not have an alibi for that time period.

The primary factor in determining a victim's time of death is the internal temperature of the body. Within the first twelve hours after death, the body cools at a rate of approximately one-and-a-half to two degrees per hour. This provides a simple mathematical equation for investigators to use to discover the time of death. Internal temperature, however, can be affected by external factors. If a body were in water, it would have cooled faster or, conversely, if heat were applied to the body it would

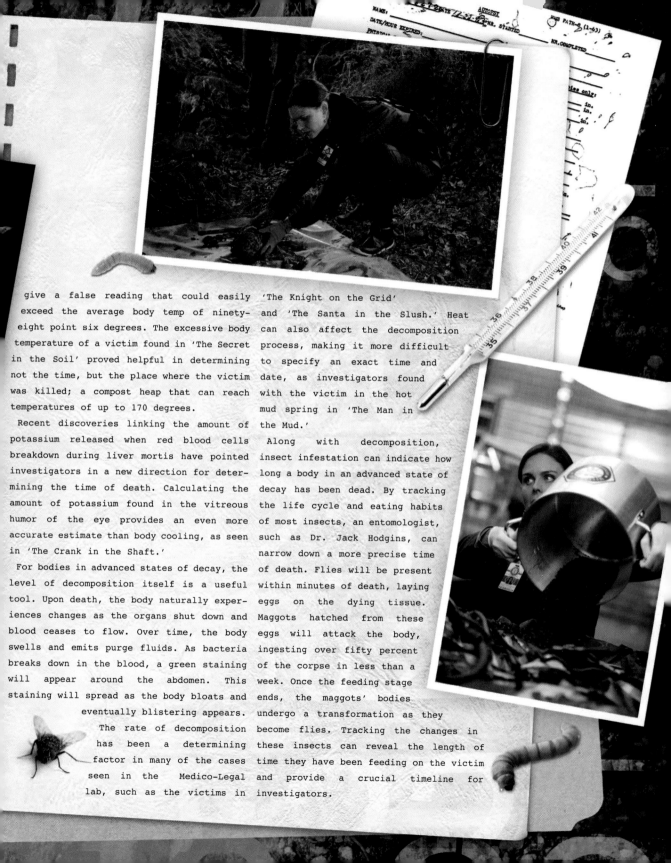

give a false reading that could easily exceed the average body temp of ninety-eight point six degrees. The excessive body temperature of a victim found in 'The Secret in the Soil' proved helpful in determining not the time, but the place where the victim was killed; a compost heap that can reach temperatures of up to 170 degrees.

Recent discoveries linking the amount of potassium released when red blood cells breakdown during liver mortis have pointed investigators in a new direction for determining the time of death. Calculating the amount of potassium found in the vitreous humor of the eye provides an even more accurate estimate than body cooling, as seen in 'The Crank in the Shaft.'

For bodies in advanced states of decay, the level of decomposition itself is a useful tool. Upon death, the body naturally experiences changes as the organs shut down and blood ceases to flow. Over time, the body swells and emits purge fluids. As bacteria breaks down in the blood, a green staining will appear around the abdomen. This staining will spread as the body bloats and eventually blistering appears.

The rate of decomposition has been a determining factor in many of the cases seen in the Medico-Legal lab, such as the victims in

'The Knight on the Grid' and 'The Santa in the Slush.' Heat can also affect the decomposition process, making it more difficult to specify an exact time and date, as investigators found with the victim in the hot mud spring in 'The Man in the Mud.'

Along with decomposition, insect infestation can indicate how long a body in an advanced state of decay has been dead. By tracking the life cycle and eating habits of most insects, an entomologist, such as Dr. Jack Hodgins, can narrow down a more precise time of death. Flies will be present within minutes of death, laying eggs on the dying tissue. Maggots hatched from these eggs will attack the body, ingesting over fifty percent of the corpse in less than a week. Once the feeding stage ends, the maggots' bodies undergo a transformation as they become flies. Tracking the changes in these insects can reveal the length of time they have been feeding on the victim and provide a crucial timeline for investigators.

THE KNIGHT ON THE GRID

WRITTEN BY NOAH HAWLEY **DIRECTED BY** DWIGHT LITTLE

SPECIAL GUEST STAR: RYAN O'NEAL (MAX KEENAN)
GUEST STARRING: JOHN FRANCIS DALEY (DR. LANCE SWEETS), PATRICIA BELCHER (CAROLINE JULIAN), BESS WOHL (AMY HOLLISTER), LEON RUSSOM (ARCHBISHOP STEPHEN WALLACE), DAVID BRISBIN (JUDGE WATKINS), CARLEASE BURKE (JOYCE HEWITT), JAMES IMMEKUS (GORMOGON'S APPRENTICE), ROXANA BRUSSO (PAROLE OFFICER ERICA DAVIS), ERIC K. GEORGE (MARK NAYLOR), RAY ABRUZZO (RAY PORTER), LOREN DEAN (RUSS BRENNAN)

- The body of a middle-aged man is found with a stab wound to the chest dealt by a double-edged blade that is later matched to a weapon in the Gormogon vault.
- The victim's patellas were removed and mailed to Dr. Brennan. Dental records identify him as Father Douglas Cooper, Vicar General to the Archbishop of Washington D.C.
- Using a tapestry from the vault as a guide, the team determines that the killer is matching the murder locations to plot points on a map of Washington D.C. One point leads to a mausoleum where a completed Widow's Son sculpture is found. The advanced age of the bones and the differences in bite marks suggest a second, older, killer.
- Another tapestry in the vault suggests that the victims fill certain roles in society, leading them to believe their next victim is a lobbyist who went on a trip to Turkey with the other victims. Jade and **sepiolite** found with the body are from the Anatolia region of Turkey.
- A number on the rib of the older skeleton leads to a safe deposit box in the vault. It contains an old key to an office in the social services building that once belonged to a man named Arthur Graves. He is likely the original Gormogon, but it will be difficult to prove as the man suffers from Alzheimer's disease and all his teeth have been pulled.

Booth and Brennan lay a trap for the serial killer, but their plan backfires when the Gormogon attempts to blow up their car with a bomb containing his master's teeth.

The special effects stunt incorporated a brief motorcycle pursuit with an explosion. "We definitely tossed that car," Kent Genzlinger proudly recalls. "We spent the day in San Pedro doing the motorcycle pursuit and explosion. It went perfectly."

This action-packed episode gave the audience many more clues into the mystery of the Gormogon killer. Furthermore, the production team were able to explore more deeply the villain they had had virtual carte blanche to do as they pleased with, right from the start. "The Gormogon Society is probably one of the least documented societies," says prop master Ian Scheibel. "If you Google 'Gormogon' most of your hits will be about *Bones*, which frees you to get creative. In

other words, we made up a bunch of cool-looking stuff that looked appropriate to an eighteenth-century, evil secret society."

That's not to say that the Gormogon storyline didn't entail a lot of research on the part of the creative team. Set decorator Kimberly Wannop relates, "It's always interesting to dress a killer's space and think about what this character is doing in here, before and after he kills. The serial killer was described as anti-everything; anti-religion, anti-mason, etc. So we found the symbols for different religions and then dressed them in the set."

The design team also looked into the Freemasons, because much of the look of the Gormogon came from his being diametrically opposed to that organization. This was clearly evident with the map of Washington D.C.—a city designed using hidden symbols of the Freemasons—

Russ: That's the most reassuring you can be? "Hey, Russ, congratulations on never killing anyone?"

Brennan: Being reassuring has never been my strong suit.

being juxtaposed to provide the Gormogon kill sites. Wannop explains, "Production designer Michael Mayer and I looked into the Masons in great detail. It's fascinating that there was—and still is—this secret society that was so influential in our country's history. The dressing in the set showed how much Gormogon hated these groups. We had religious statues that we made into demons, Mason paintings that he had altered. We had every type of religious book in there—the Bible, Koran, etc.—that he had degraded."

Wannop describes how the entire vault was set up with an eye into the mind of their killer while meeting the needs of the production. "Michael built an altar in the middle of the space for Gormogon's sacrifices," she says. "The entrance of the vault is his 'living space' with tons of books and maps. Since the setting of his lair is a bank vault, you have a lot of that steel and

marble around you—very cold—so the furniture in the room was minimal to make it uncomfortable. There was a huge gothic chair in the entrance and vintage trunks throughout the space to evoke the question: what could he be keeping inside them? The walls had hundreds of security boxes for clues.

"The main space with the silver skeleton and the altar was his 'working space.' Along the sides of the vault I set up a painting space, and then in the rear is an old wooden table full of old wines and a silver place setting. When the vault gets moved to the Jeffersonian, we took all of the small items and tagged them with evidence tags, which progressed through the season to show that the evidence was all being cataloged." That vault provided an additional set for the cast and crew to work in, and gave the show an even more ominous feel as the storyline progressed.

Sepiolite: A clay mineral.

'Low is a Height' by Great Northern, *Trading Twilight for Daylight*
'Sail Away' by Madrugada, *The Deep End*

THE SANTA IN THE SLUSH

WRITTEN BY ELIZABETH BENJAMIN & SCOTT WILLIAMS
DIRECTED BY JEFF WOOLNOUGH

SPECIAL GUEST STAR: RYAN O'NEAL (MAX KEENAN)
GUEST STARRING: PATRICIA BELCHER (CAROLINE JULIAN), DAVID DELUISE (JEFF MANTELL), REGINALD VEL JOHNSON (DALE OWENS), ERNIE GRUNWALD (FRED SPIVAK), DONOVAN SCOTT (LARRY), DAVID DOTY (RALPH HARLEY), DAVID ACKERT (MARTY MOUSSA), BESS WOHL (AMY HOLLISTER), ALESSANDRA TORRESANI (TEENAGE GIRL ELF), KACIE BORROWMAN (LITTLE PERSON ELF), LOREN DEAN (RUSS BRENNAN)

- The decomposing body of a bearded man in a Santa suit is found in a sewer. The gloves of the victim's costume provide a fingerprint matching a school district employee named Kristopher Kringle.
- Booth finds a hidden stash of money in the victim's apartment. The landlord leads investigators to Temp Time Agency, where Kringle was their most successful Santa.
- Damage to the left side of the skull suggests a strong blow to the temporal lobe. Localized staining on the bone suggests the superficial temporal artery was ruptured, making the blow to the head fatal. There is a faint crescent shaped margin near the **sphenosquamosal suture**.
- Maggots in the Santa suit fed on bird's nest soup. The evidence leads to the murder scene, an alley outside a restaurant in Chinatown. Wallets are found in a nearby dumpster.
- Metal shavings in the wound indicate that the weapon was made of brass. The crescent shape suggests it was a bell similar to the ones used by the temp agency. Blood residue is found on one bell, but all the workers share the prop.
- Based on the suspicion that Kringle rolled in the bird's nest soup with his attacker, Brennan conducts a nasal experiment for the scent of the soup. She finds it on the suit of one of the Santas, a pickpocket that killed the victim when confronted with evidence of his crime.

Brennan talks to Caroline Julian about her father's wish to have a family holiday in jail. The federal prosecutor agrees to the plan, so long as Brennan meets one condition: she must share a kiss with Booth under the mistletoe.

"The guiding principle in TV is to fulfill audience expectations in a way they don't expect," Hart Hanson says, explaining how they approached the all-important first kiss between Brennan and Booth. "We take that very seriously. Everyone's very anxiously awaiting the consummation of their romantic life. The most stressful thing about the show is tracing this storyline in a satisfying way. The kiss was a way of letting off romantic pressure."

"We just felt that we had to get them to touch each other in some way," Stephen Nathan agrees. "And this seemed to be a very fun, very benign way to do it. Both characters wanted to do it, although they would never say that. But neither one had responsibility for the kiss. It was a way to get them to kiss through a way to get them to kiss through Caroline Julian that absolved them of all responsibility for that kiss, but it gave the audience the knowledge that they really liked that kiss. It seemed to be an ideal way to handle that next tiny step in their relationship that everyone was pining for."

The kiss got a lot of play in the press before it even happened; the internet making secrets almost impossible to keep in the film and TV industry. Unlike many other shows, the producers on *Bones* are happy to release some spoilers, so long as they can control the story. "The fact that Booth and Brennan kissing existed meant that Fox was going to promote that element of the show," Stephen Nathan concedes. "It was such a promoteable element and would get so many viewers to watch, and even attract new viewers, there was no way we were going to hide it. The only thing that we *could* hide was how exactly it came about and what it meant. That's really what you want to tune in to see."

Caroline Julian: Because you're all "Dr. Brennan" and "Special Agent Seeley Booth" and it's Christmas and I have a puckish side that will not be denied.

But would a kiss borne out of blackmail satisfy? Emily Deschanel believes that it did have an important impact on her character and the Booth/Brennan relationship. "Even though the kiss came out of blackmail, I think both Booth and Brennan enjoyed it a little too much and it forced them to acknowledge their feelings on some level. Certainly not to each other, but maybe to themselves."

The kiss does result in Brennan's family spending the holiday together. Booth also gets his Christmas wish when Parker runs away to see his dad. Father and son then surprise Brennan's family by hooking up a Christmas tree outside the jail so they can have an unconventionally traditional Christmas together.

Sphenosquamosal suture: A cranial suture located between the sphenoid bone at the base of the skull and the squama of the temporal bone.

'A Holly Jolly Christmas' by Burl Ives, *Rudolph the Red-Nosed Reindeer Soundtrack*

'Santa Claus is Comin' to Town' by Peggy Lee, *Christmas With Peggy Lee*

We Now Interrupt Our Regularly Scheduled Program

STRIKE

The third season of *Bones* will go down in the books as the year of the writers' strike. The job action called by the Writers Guild of America East and Writers Guild of America West labor unions had a dramatic effect on the production of the show, due to the abrupt work stoppage in the middle of the year. It complicated the overall story of the Gormogon killer, but it affected other major plot points as well.

The writers' strike was set to begin on November 5, 2007. At the time it was announced, the producers, cast, and crew of *Bones* were already headlong into the season. Scripts were turned in and continued to be turned in until the official walkout. Hart Hanson had figured on wrapping production with a powerful episode in 'The Wanna-be in the Weeds.' But things didn't go exactly according to plan. "We tried to guess where the strike might fall," Hanson notes. "But it actually fell just before that episode started shooting." That didn't stop the script from being filmed. It just meant that the writers could not be involved.

"It's hard to stop mid-stream," laments Stephan Nathan. "We had to walk away even from editing the show and doing final post. The people who remained did a very good job, but it's hard to wash your hands of something that means so much to you during that time."

While Hanson, Nathan and the rest of the writing staff were on the picket line, the remaining episodes were in the capable hands of those left behind. Barry Josephson notes, "I have terrific group of other non-writer producers who were able to make the process go as quickly and efficiently as possible, but it's not ideal. Television truly has brilliant directors and great actors and there are great people working on our show creatively on every level, but the complete driver and the complete vision of the show is the showrunner. You need to run into his office three, four, five times a day. Without the person with the true vision—the sole vision—of the show, you're sort of headless."

"You were left the script, but you couldn't work on the script," Steve Beers explains. "It became difficult from a production standpoint because you couldn't alter the script. You couldn't walk down to a writer/producer or the showrunner and go, 'We're $55,000 over budget because we're doing this and if we could do this we would get the same creative intent, but save the $55,000.' Basically what you had to do is turn yourself inside out to shoot the script that had been left in development. It was really nerve-wracking."

Twelve full episodes were filmed before the production ran out of scripts and was forced to close down. One additional episode, 'Player Under Pressure,' had been held over from the prior season, giving the network a total of thirteen episodes. Once those episodes were completed, the cast and crew went on hiatus for several months. If that had been the full season, the writers had left them with a powerful ending: Booth being shot at the end of 'The Wanna-be in the Weeds.'

But that was not the end. What no one had anticipated was that the network would hold some of the episodes from airing. Keeping hope alive that the writers' strike would be resolved in time to salvage the season, Fox put the series on hiatus after 'The Santa in the Slush,'

the romantic "cliff-hanger" of Booth and Brennan's kiss intended to whet the audience's appetite until the series did return. This left 'The Baby in the Bough,' 'The Man in the Mud,' 'The Wanna-be in the Weeds,' and 'Player Under Pressure' in the can and on hold.

The strike ended on February 12, 2008 and the writers immediately went back to work. But the network threw another monkey wrench into the plan by ordering two more episodes for season three. They also decided to film a handful of episodes that would be held over for season four. While it was a positive sign that the network has so much faith in the show that they wanted as many episodes as possible, it meant a scramble for the writers. They immediately had to figure out a plan to save Booth's life, hold the trial of Brennan's father, wrap up the Gormogon storyline, and set the stories in motion for the fourth season.

And, just for fun, they took the production to England, too.

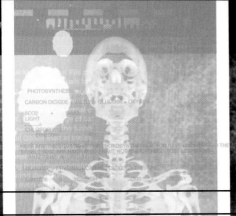

THE MAN IN THE MUD

WRITTEN BY JANET TAMARO   DIRECTED BY SCOTT LAUTANEN

GUEST STARRING: ABIGAIL SPENCER (PHILLIPA FITZ), M.C. GAINEY (BRAXTON SMALLS), WINGS HAUSER (LENNY FITZ), CHRIS WILLIAM MARTIN (GARTH JODREY), CHANNON ROE (DANNY FITZ), SENTA MOSES (APRIL PRESA), DARLENA TEJEIRO (F.B.I. MOTOR TECH OPAL WARNEKE), ANDREW LAWRENCE (TIM), ALICIA ZIEGLAR (CHANDLER), CHRISTOPHER MAY (PARK RANGER)

- A couple in search of romance finds the remains of a body in a muddy hot spring. A rendering of the victim matches the image of motorcycle racer Tripp Goddard.
- The victim was struck in the rear of the skull multiple times by a square pipe, possibly a pry bar. There is also a vertical impaction fracture to the **glabella** and **frontonasal suture** from a different weapon, suggesting the victim was attacked from both the front and behind.
- One of the suspects, Danny Fitz, has a fatal motorcycle accident during the investigation. An examination of his bike reveals it was tampered with.
- When Goddard's truck is located, the pry bar is also found. Glass in the victim's frontal wound is matched to the truck's side mirror suggesting the victim hit the mirror after being struck in the back of the head by the pry bar.
- The pattern of the blood spatter on the pry bar suggests that the killer "choked up" to be able to swing the weapon, signifying that the killer was likely female.
- It is determined that Danny Fitz's sister, Phillipa, killed Goddard after her father made a deal with the victim that should have been reserved for family. She also rigged Goddard's bike, which accidentally resulted in her own brother's death. Though the evidence is not enough to stand in court, Booth arrests the woman so that everyone, including her father, will know what she's done.

In the ongoing analysis of the Booth/Brennan working relationship, Dr. Sweets suspects that his subjects only share their personal lives with one another when those lives intersect with their work. His suggestion that they have nothing in common outside of their jobs annoys both Booth and Brennan. To explore this side of their relationship, Sweets suggests that they accompany him and his girlfriend, April, on an evening out that has nothing to do with work—and

sounds suspiciously like a double date.

In spite of the many fun-filled adventures Booth might consider being up for—bowling for example—the foursome end up taking a pottery class together. The night out takes an unexpected turn when Dr. Sweets's relationship is the one that is aversely affected, while Booth and Brennan actually enjoy themselves. The double-date subplot that was originally focused on Booth and Brennan's relationship ultimately gave the audience a deeper understanding of the show's newest character, Dr. Lance Sweets.

As of 'The Santa in the Slush,' John Francis Daley had become a regular member of the cast and, as Stephen Nathan recalls, the actor and the character were quickly absorbed into the production. "Sweets is somebody who is smart and mature intellectually, but is still inexperienced in the world. He has that kind of innocence of youth coupled with an intellectual maturity that we don't normally see in a character. The internal conflict is so greatly realized by John. It really was natural bringing Sweets into the group. We found ourselves writing for

Booth: I hate when you do this.

Dr. Sweets: Do what?

Booth: You don't talk.

Dr. Sweets: Sometimes you hate when I talk, so it's a double-edged sword.

him with real ease. You just don't know how a new character's going to fit in and it was just effortless. It seems as if he belonged there always."

John Francis Daley had a bit of an inauspicious welcome to the show in this episode. The actor admits he would have had more fun filming 'The Man in the Mud' if it weren't for the mud that got in the man. During the pottery scene, Sweets annoys his girlfriend to the point that she flings clay at him. It's a humorous moment that became a little less endearing when the clay accidentally got in his eye. The clay itself wasn't as bad as the process to clean it out, which required his eye to be numbed. "I had to go to the medic and it became this whole thing that I didn't want it to become," Daley explains, citing the understandably cautious reaction at the studio. "They have to take every precaution necessary. The actual numbing of my eye was way worse than the clay being thrown into it. It was a very strange experience. I might as well have gotten Lasik eye surgery in that time!"

Glabella: Smooth part of the forehead above and between the eyebrows.

Frontonasal suture: The point where the frontal and two nasal bones connect in the skull.

'Get it Right' by Mink, *Mink*
'Skinny Penny' by The Stereotypes, *3*

PLAYER UNDER PRESSURE

WRITTEN BY JANET TAMARO   DIRECTED BY JESSICA LANDAW

GUEST STARRING: JAMES BLACK (CHIEF JACK CUTLER), JAMIL WALKER (COLBY PAGE), DANIEL ROEBUCK (GEORGE FRANCIS), MICHAEL MCGRADY (COACH MORSE), ERIK VON DETTEN (ED DEKKER), WHITNEY ANDERSON (DALLAS VERONA), MEKIA COX (CELESTE CUTLER), MICHELLE PAGE (JUSTINE BERRY), TAYLOR KINNEY (JIMMY FIELDS), STEPHANIE CHARLES (KAMARIA MANNING)

- The crushed remains of star college basketball player, RJ Manning, are found beneath the bleachers of the school court.
- The victim's skull shows evidence of powdering from multiple strikes, suggesting he was dead before being crushed by the bleachers. Later, an indentation in the skull leads investigators to the murder weapon: a free weight in the school weight room.
- Excess **synovial fluid** in the victim's joints suggests that Manning had gonorrhea.
- The **tarsus** of a cockroach found on the body is covered in blue lipstick. Matching lipstick residue is also discovered in the victim's shorts. Esophageal mucus found in the victim's hair posits a scenario where the victim was killed and spat upon while being serviced by a person wearing blue lipstick.
- The lipstick is matched to a promotional line sold to cheerleaders, indicating that Manning was with a cheerleader at the time of his death. A DNA swab links cheerleader Celeste Cutler to the victim.
- When the DNA is not a match for the mucus found in the victim's hair, CODIS links it to campus police captain, Jack Cutler. The former sports star was enraged when he found his daughter with the victim and killed Manning after his daughter fled the scene.

In a similar way to 'The Boy in the Time Capsule,' Booth is presented with another case that allows him to reminisce about his youth. The mysterious death of a basketball star takes him back to his own college days as a jock, while Brennan has trouble coming to grips with how much emphasis sports has at the university over academics. Booth takes offense to the dismissive way Brennan describes the sociological aspects of boys playing team sports, until she reminds him that he is

not a man who falls easily into generalizations.

'Player Under Pressure' is one of those fun episodes that everyone in the production enjoyed working on, in spite of the fact that it had its fair share of challenges typical to television production, as well as one tragic complication. Originally filmed toward the end of the second season the episode was under a tight schedule as things always seem to be when the production nears the end of a season. This presented an interesting challenge for first assistant director Kent Genzlinger, but it was a test his experience in television had adequately prepared him for. "We had to rehearse the cheerleaders' routine and we were on a very tight schedule," he recalls. "I actually had to bring them in the morning of the scene. Having worked with cheerleaders before, I told my second A.D., 'I just need central casting to bring in a dozen cheerleaders and at least four or five of them that are from the same cheerleading team with a cheerleading captain.'"

With those simple instructions, the cheerleaders were cast. When they came

in on the day of filming, Genzlinger then received the expected question of what were they going to rehearse? There was a scene when the cheerleaders performed, but no one had worked out what cheer the extras—and two guest actresses—were supposed to do. Genzlinger, who had worked with cheerleaders before on the short-lived Spelling television series *Heaven Help Us*, met with the cheerleading captain and gave her instructions. "I said, 'Here's our two actresses. Here's six other girls you haven't worked with. Go into this other gym and show them the routines you guys know.' They walked away and the second A.D. said to me, 'I don't understand.' And I said, 'Don't worry. You put twelve cheerleaders in a room and they're going to be doing the same routines in fifteen minutes.' And sure enough, a half an hour

later they all had the same routine down perfectly. It was very funny to see them not know each other, but half an hour later come out as if they were *Bring It On* part three. You get the right cheerleading captain and those girls are going to whip that stuff out very quickly."

The minor production issues paled in comparison to what occurred on the campus of Virginia Tech on April 16, 2007. On that date, an armed student killed thirty-two people and wounded numerous others. Though the real life horror bore no resemblance to the fictional episode, the producers and Fox were understandably concerned. Stephen Nathan explains, "I think [we were due to air] a week after the tragedy and there was just no way we could focus a show on a murder at a university at that point. It just made us very, very uncomfortable. It seemed

Synovial fluid: A lubricant found in the cavities of the joints.
Tarsus: A group of bones found in the foot of tetrapods.

'Uprising Down Under' by Sam Roberts, *Chemical City*

unfair to the victims and to everyone involved; everyone who was a witness to it, everyone who suffered through that. It was something that we quickly decided to move to the next season." Moving the episode from one season to the next was easy enough to do for the main plot. Nothing within the case of the murdered basketball player took place in a specific time period. The same could not be said for the subplot.

The originally filmed episode, 'Player Under Pressure' included a B-story that played a significant role of the mini-arc in which Hodgins decides to ask Angela to marry him with a series of ill-advised attempts at proposing. Being that it would

now air a year later, those scenes had to be scrapped. Co-executive producer Steve Beers explains, "Because it aired after the standing at the altar situation, we had to take aspects of that story out and change them with other aspects of where their relationship was in season three. It wasn't as harrowing as it could have been because it was basically the two actors, so it was an easier arc to manipulate. When I say 'easy' I'm not one of the writers. But it wasn't that bad from a production standpoint."

Producer Jan DeWitt confirms that the production aspects of reshooting those scenes were fairly standard. "We looked back at the photos and records we kept from

the episode to recreate the characters' looks and situations, and then reshot the scenes on the same day we were shooting a season three episode. During a season, episodes continually change and need to be adjusted, so we were able to fit the reshoot into our normal organization."

The old scenes were removed (though they would later be available in the season three DVD set) and replaced with another humorous take on the Angela/Hodgins relationship. Angela grows uncomfortable when Cam asks her to pass a work-related message along to Hodgins. She feels that it crosses the line of mixing the personal and professional. Cam counters by showing Angela a video of her and Hodgins having sex in the storage area, which was caught on tape. Cam's point is made and Angela promises to be more professional herself. Though, in an amusing aside, she and Hodgins are impressed by the quality of the video they made.

Brennan: You're a smart girl. Why didn't you wear a condom?

Justine. I do! ...Most of the time.

Brennan. You know what. I made a mistake. She is not a smart girl. This is a terrible university.

This new subplot fit very nicely into the new season as Angela and Hodgins had previously discovered that a museum filled with artifacts could provide a wealth of places to explore the sexual side of their relationship. Though that video was never seen onscreen, it was definitely heard. But the question remains of whether or not the producers had used the sounds from a previously filmed romantic scene or if they had brought in sound effects. Certainly the actors aren't sure, as Michaela Conlin denies providing the soundtrack. "That was not us, unless they took it from... You know I never really asked that. I mean I certainly didn't loop anything. I don't think TJ did either. I don't recall looping anything, unless they pulled it from a prior romp in the sack that we had. But no, that wasn't us."

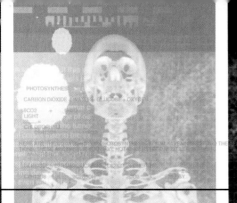

THE BABY IN THE BOUGH

WRITTEN BY KARINE ROSENTHAL   **DIRECTED BY** IAN TOYNTON

GUEST STARRING: TOM WILSON (CHIP BARNETT), AUSTIN O'BRIEN (JIMMY GRANT), BECKY WAHLSTROM (CAROL GRANT), CAMERON DYE (LOU TAYLOR), JAMES LASHLY (PAUL), SHEILA SHAW (DOROTHY), JAMES C. VICTOR (RICH), STEVE SEAGREN (SHERIFF DELPY), FRANK CLEM (EARL DELANCY), RONALD WILLIAM LAWRENCE (TERRY)

- A burned out convertible is found on a West Virginia highway with the charred body of a woman behind the wheel and a baby in a car seat perched in a tree.
- **Strontium** in the bone and particulate matter collected from the car, lead to a small town where the baby is recognized as the son of Meg Taylor, an employee at the Fallbrook Rubber Company.
- A key retrieved from the baby leads to a safe deposit box containing a gun wrapped in a rag. DNA from burned skin lining the trigger reveals that the shooter was male. Bone from the frontal bone is found in the barrel indicating that the gun was fired at point blank range at the victim's head.
- A bloodstained duffel found in a coalmine belongs to rubber company accountant, Dave Shepard. His DNA is matched to the bloody duffel and the bone fragments in the gun, making him a second victim.
- Data from a crushed flash drive found in Shepard's duffel reveals an internal audit for the rubber company that shows a different set numbers than those reported to corporate headquarters.
- Silica, sulfur compounds, and synthetic rubber found on the gun suggest it was fired at the rubber recycling plant. Tiny bone fragments are discovered in the mulch made from tires. The plant manager, Chip Barnett, is found fleeing town and admits to killing Taylor. She had witnessed Barnett murdering Shepard who caught him doctoring the accounts.

Booth is surprised to learn exactly how profitable Brennan is as an author when she expresses uncertainty about what to do with the income from her book and movie deals. Their conversation is temporarily tabled when they find a baby at a crime scene. The child becomes Brennan's ward after the little guy swallows a piece of evidence. At first, Brennan is uncomfortable around the small human, but she eventually bonds with the boy who hails from Hunstville, West Virginia, a small town which is dying out.

The poor financial situation of Huntsville cuts to the heart of the crime in this episode, making the town on the verge of collapse a central character. To find the perfect East Coast small town to act as Huntsville, location manager Deborah Laub only had to travel about an hour from the *Bones* stages to a place with a long Hollywood history. "'The Baby in the Bough' was filmed in the small town of Piru in eastern Ventura County," she explains. "It has been used as a film location as early as 1910 for the silent movie *Ramona* starring Mary Pickford. It still has only about 1200 residents and 400 small homes. The entire downtown area of the town is only two short blocks long with only one significant intersection. There are no stoplights, no palm trees, and only a few small businesses."

Brennan is so touched by the situation that she uses her own money to have the bridge leading into the town

Brennan: Phalanges! Phalanges, phalanges, phalanges! Dancing phalanges! Dancing phalanges!

repaired, putting it back on the tourist route. The town is saved and the baby is returned to his late mother's friends to be raised. Booth tries to convince Brennan to use some of her excess cash to buy a house in the town so she can visit the child. This episode would also prove important to the development of Brennan's character and her quest to become a mother in the season four episode, 'The Critic in the Cabernet.' Certainly, the fans would refer back to it when questioning the decision before the episode even aired. But Emily Dechanel sees it as perfectly normal for Brennan to grow in that way. "What's important to someone one year may mean nothing the next," she explains. "I always look for the contradictions in a character. It's what makes them human. That's what I love about this show. The characters are always human. This episode is also notable for Brennan's very maternal reaction to the child and Deschanel's stunning performance of the "dancing phalanges" while trying to entertain the pre-verbal infant.

Brennan isn't the only one moved by the little guy, however. Hodgins freaks a little when Angela admits she wants a million kids. Logically, she knows she will have to settle for less, but just how many is up for discussion, even when Angela considers what effect multiple births will have on her body.

Strontium: A soft, silver-white metal of the alkaline earth series.

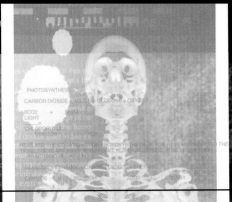

THE VERDICT IN THE STORY

WRITTEN BY CHRISTOPHER AMBROSE **DIRECTED BY** JEANNOT SZWARC

SPECIAL GUEST STAR: RYAN O'NEAL (MAX KEENAN)
GUEST STARRING: PATRICIA BELCHER (CAROLINE JULIAN), ERNIE HUDSON (DAVID BARRON), EUGENE BYRD (DR. CLARK EDISON), GEORGE WYNER (JUDGE MARCUS HADDOES), RYAN CUTRONA (F.B.I. DEPUTY DIRECTOR ROBERT KIRBY), LOREN DEAN (RUSS BRENNAN)

The following is a compilation of the pertinent facts in the case against Max Keenan for the murder of F.B.I. Deputy Director Kirby:

• Cause of death was a sharp instrument that entered at the rear of the skull and terminated at the mandible, cutting the carotid artery in the process. Small traces of copper were found in the **mylohyoid line** of the mandible. The murder weapon matched a sharpened pipe the defendant used once before in prison. It was found among the remains of the victim.

• DNA from the blood pool found in Dr. Brennan's apartment was a match for the victim. Particles of soil found at the murder site matches samples found on the rooftop where the body was found and Our Lady of Angles Cemetery where the defendant had been seen earlier in the day.

• Striations on the bone confirm that the murder weapon was a sharp-tipped instrument matching the diameter of the pipe. However, when red dye is applied to the wound and viewed at 120 magnification, micro-fractures are revealed on the bone. This indicates that the hilt of the murder weapon struck the bone. As the pipe has no hilt, it is disqualified as the murder weapon. A ceremonial knife in Dr. Brennan's apartment matches the description of the true weapon and is entered into evidence.

All of Brennan's coworkers are witnesses for the prosecution in her father's trial for the murder of F.B.I. Deputy Director Kirby, which presents a challenge for Caroline Julian who needs to prep the team.

"She's the great mouthpiece," Hart Hanson says, of Caroline Julian as portrayed by Patricia Belcher. "Every once in a while she gets to say to these characters what the audience wants to say to them. In the trial of Brennan's dad, she just tells them: 'Get it together. Use your brains.' I was there on the day Patricia shot that scene because I wrote that dialogue and I wanted to see if it was too many words. She stumbled in rehearsal and I thought, 'Maybe I should cut some of this.' But she said, 'No, no. I can do it.' And

she did: when the cameras were on she didn't falter. When it was over, and the director yelled cut, the cast and crew just started clapping."

The Squints have a hard time putting up evidence against Brennan's father in court. Angela flat out refuses to testify and is held in contempt. Brennan brings in forensic anthropologist Clark Edison to review the evidence, and he finds a flaw in Zack's usually meticulous work. Eric Millegan recalls that it was an important moment for his character. "Once I got my doctorate the writers said they were going to have me go in and go opposite Dr. Brennan. So it was really exciting when we did that. It's fun to play court scenes. It was fun to play an angle of the character where he's not perfect."

Brennan, by way of the defense lawyer, forces Booth to admit that the facts support that she also could have committed the crime. It is enough reasonable doubt to get Max an acquittal and reunite the fractured family. "I find the dynamics in Brennan's family fascinating," notes Emily Deschanel. "Her father is essentially a murderer; basically

Caroline Julian: (To Booth) …lose the "Cocky" belt buckle. (To Hodgins) No badges saying, "Resist authority" or "The truth is out there." (To Zack) Do not cut your own hair the day before a trial. (To Angela) Ugly up a little. The plain women on the jury hate you. (To Sweets) Use your fully grown-up words. (To Cam) Eat. Last time your stomach was growling louder than your testimony.

a bad guy. But he does bad things for good reasons. That's been something Brennan has learned to see: the gray in-betweens of life. She loves her father, but doesn't approve of what he's done. Yet she feels compelled to keep him out of jail."

Out in the light of day, after the trial, the team comes back together. Everyone, it seems, will live happily ever after.

Steve Beers explains that this final scene was filmed at one of his favorite locations the show has visited so far. "It was neat because it was such an interior

episode that we found a way to get outside to the other side of city hall, a side that's never shot. The end of the scene, which had a great deal of production value, is really not a dialogue scene. It's more body language. It's people coming out and reattaching themselves to the fact that they were on different sides of that situation and the trial and somehow their friendships and their honesty with each other survived it and they were bonding again under that wonderful federal architecture. It was just great."

Mylohyoid line: A ridge on the lower jaw that is the origin point for the muscle that runs from the mandible to the hyoid bone.

'Fountain' by Sara Lov, *Bones (Original Television Soundtrack)*

THE WANNA-BE IN THE WEEDS

WRITTEN BY *JOSH BERMAN*   DIRECTED BY *GORDON C. LONSDALE*

GUEST STARRING: *JENNIFER HASTY (PAM NUNAN), CORBIN ALLRED (ADAM MATTHEWS), KENT FAULCON (DR. JASON BERGMAN), ETHAN PHILLIPS (JERRY LINCOLN), IAN REED KESLER (CHRIS CALABASA), GEOFF MEED (DAX), JOSHUA WEINSTEIN (MITCHELL), JOHN BOBEK (DRIVER)*

- Human remains are found in the brush along a rural roadside after a road worker ran over a body with a mulching machine, breaking every bone in the process.
- Traces of tea, honey, and the remains of a throat lozenge are found in the victim's stomach. Dental records identify the victim as Tommy Sour, an aspiring singer who was reported missing two weeks earlier by his neighbor.
- The C5 vertebrae is shaved just under the hyoid, suggesting someone slit the victim's throat, but there are no serrations from a knife. A guitar string is initially believed to be the murder weapon. There is also a fracture to the chin.
- Blood tests reveal that the victim was infected with E. coli hours before his death. The CDC last reported an E. coli outbreak at the Checker Box restaurant in Virginia, where the victim regularly performed on open mic night.
- An elemental trace on the hyoid and C5 vertebrae reveals a composite including **phyllosilicate** minerals and **aluminium oxide** silver particulates, like those found in a certain brand of sculpting clay. That clay was recently shipped to the sculptor who lived next door to the victim. Blood residue is found on a clay-cutting wire in the sculptor's apartment. The suspect admits that he killed the victim because the man's singing was too distracting to the artistic process.

The music intensive episode was highlighted by the cameo appearance of a pair of *American Idol* castoffs, Ace Young and Brandon Rogers. But they were far from the only notables to contribute their vocal abilities to the episode. Both Emily Deschanel and Broadway veteran, Eric Millegan, had the chance to show off their pipes, both onstage and in the lab.

"They talked about that from day one," Eric Millegan admits. "When we were shooting the pilot and I told Hart that I do musical theatre. He was like, 'We'll have to have you sing on the show!'" Millegan was understandably skeptical about this promise as it didn't seem to fit his

character, especially in the early days of the series. But Hart Hanson was insistent that they would find a way to make it work, and eventually they did.

"The script actually said that I sang 'Aquarius,'" Millegan notes, "because I sang the solo at the beginning of 'Aquarius' in a concert in New York about eight years ago. Hart had heard a recording of it online, so when he wrote the script he wanted Zack to sing that. But they couldn't get the rights to it. About two days before we shot the scene, the guy who gets the rights to the music came up to me and said, 'You're singing 'Love is a Many Splendored Thing.'" Millegan knew the song, but he immediately went on the internet to find the lyrics and listen to different arrangements on iTunes. He used what he found to put together a little cut of the song and was ready to perform for the cameras.

Emily Deschanel did not have the experience that her costar possessed, so she was a little more tentative about her rousing rendition of 'Girls Just Want to Have Fun' that closed the episode. As Deschanel explains, "Originally in the script the singing was described as being very impressive. Brennan was supposed to

Zack: My regimen is easily completed in my apartment: treadmill for thirty minutes, a hundred sit-ups, push-ups and leg lifts and twenty minutes of free weights. I'm deceptively strong.

Cam: I'm deceived.

'blow everyone away.' It really made me nervous. I have sung before, but I am not a singer. They also chose a song that's not great for my voice and we couldn't change it because the writers went on strike."

Despite this, Deschanel was excited by the song choice. "I must say, though, that Cindy Lauper was a huge idol of mine as a child. I *loved* her and I love that song. I wasn't trying not to sing well, but I'm happy the way it came out. The most important thing for me was for Brennan to commit to the song completely. It's hard to sing in public. It was freeing to face that

fear, for myself, and for Brennan."

But Brennan was about to face a much larger fear as she sang onstage: One of the suspects in the investigation makes an emotional connection with Booth. Though Dr. Sweets tries to warn them that the woman, Pam, is a dangerous stalker, they mock him for his concern. He is quickly proven correct when Pam shoots at Brennan while she sings. Booth crosses into the path of the bullet to protect his partner and Brennan grabs the gun before another shot can be fired. But the damage is already done: Booth has been shot.

Phyllosilicate: A mineral containing silicon and oxygen.

Aluminium oxide: A chemical compound of aluminium and oxygen.

Karaoke selections include: **'I'm a Slave 4 U,' 'Biggest Part of Me,' 'Working 9 to 5,' 'Talk to the Animals,' 'Far Away,' 'Piano Man,' 'Corner of the Sky,' 'The Second Time Around,' 'Love is a Many Splendored Thing,' 'Girls Just Want to Have Fun'**

The Gormogon Serial Killer

F.B.I. investigators first encountered the killer who became known as Gormogon when the skull of one of his victims fell from a freeway overpass. Clues in the remains found by the staffers in the Medico-Legal department of the Jeffersonian led investigators to a bank vault where the killer had set up a ritualistic shrine. In that vault, a silver skeleton was found. The silver bones were being replaced individually with actual bones from the killer's victims.

At the time of discovery, the skeleton consisted of ten bones from six separate victims:

Victim 1: Fibula and tibia of the right leg.

Victim 2: Left femur.

Victim 3: Manubrium

Victim 4: Gladiolus

Victim 5: "Floating" rib

Victim 6: Three phalanges and one metacarpal. Pressure indicators were consistent with years of violin practice, indicating that these bones belonged to the body at the core of the initial investigation.

The skeleton was posed in the attitude of what the ancient Greeks called "Pharmakos," which means "scapegoat" or "sacrifice." Most secret societies have this figure deep in their origins. To Freemasons, it's known as "The Widow's Son." The first identified victim, Gavin Nichols, lost his father when he was twelve, making him the son of a widow. An Ancient Greek phrase burned into the back of the vault door was originally translated as: "Will no one help the Widow's Son?" However, there is an alternate translation for the quote that reveals a very different message: "No one will help the Widow's Son."

The vault and its complete contents were transported to the Jeffersonian lab. The design of the relics suggested that the killer was a member of the Gormogon Society, a supposedly extinct group dedicated to eradicating secret societies like the Freemasons and Illuminati in Europe in the early eighteenth century. The Gormogons championed the ideal that humanity should be free of these pernicious influences.

Of the many relics in the vault, one that proved the most useful in providing clues was a tapestry representing the figure of Barabbas, a murderer and rapist

Report No.

Subject.

condemned to death in New Testament Jerusalem. Pontius Pilate offered both Barabbas and Jesus to the mob and said, "Whom should I crucify?" The Gormogons believe the descendents of Barabbas started the first secret societies and see him as an enduring symbol of all that is backwards, upside-down, and inside out. Traditionally, when the figure of Barabbas is found on a Gormogon relic, it is a sign to interpret the message backwards or upside-down.

Numbers on the tapestry are a simple alphanumeric code with each digit corresponding to a letter: Civitas Capitolium or "Capitol City." Considering that city planners laid out Washington D.C. in accordance with Masonic symbols, the presence of Barabbas on the tapestry indicated that a map of D.C. should be read upside down and backwards. This revealed key points where the victim's bodies were found, as well as a nursing home that turned out to be the residence of the serial killer's presumed master. Considering the history of the Gormogon, it was determined that investigators were dealing with a master and apprentice situation, whereupon each master

created one of the skeletal sculptures while training an apprentice. When it was complete, the master retired, while the apprentice became The Master and began his own project.

Symbols on another tapestry in the vault include images of key archetypes that extend from the seventeenth century: The Architect, The Martyr, The Orator, The Musician, The Bishop, The Corruptor, The Scientist, The Hermit, The Teacher, and The Judge. It was determined that victims were chosen who matched these titles and were being killed in the order of a counterclockwise position on the tapestry.

Near the end of the investigation, the Gormogon made a set of dentures out of human canine teeth. Canines are a symbol of the wolf, which appears on the Gormogon tapestry in the vault. Certain sects revere the wolf as a symbol of freedom and as a representative of the forces who will "deliver us from persecution." It was believed that the killer convinced himself that he was doing important work to rid the world of people and secret societies that were unjustly controlling their lives.

THE PAIN IN THE HEART

WRITTEN BY *HART HANSON & STEPHEN NATHAN*
DIRECTED BY *ALLAN KROEKER*

GUEST STARRING: PATRICIA BELCHER (CAROLINE JULIAN), DONNIE JEFFCOAT (HOWIE MADISON), GRAHAM MILLER (GRAD STUDENT #1), ALAIN UY (GRAD STUDENT #2), MEGAN PAUL (GRAD STUDENT #3)

- Dr. Brennan receives a package containing a human jawbone with two silver screws. DNA from the tooth sockets matches lobbyist Ray Porter.
- The presence of tooth marks on the bone suggest that it is from the Gormogon killer, but the markings indicate the cannibal was wearing dentures. Zack finds **polymethyl-methacrylate** on the mandible, suggesting homemade dentures. Zack and Hodgins attempt to recreate the dentures. The resulting explosion later proves to be cover for the theft of the Gormogon skeleton.
- Trace elements from the mandible reveal a high lead level in the water used to boil the victim's bone, revealing the location of the killer's neighborhood.
- The jawbone was treated with ultraviolet light which is part of the standard procedure for skeletal remains placed in the Jeffersonian's bone storage unit. Several bones from the body of a man are located in storage. DNA in the bones matches the lobbyist that disappeared. A series of skulls are also found with all the canines removed.
- Brennan determines that the markings on the bones came from dentures made from real canine teeth, not the false dentures Zack had identified. Knowing that was not a mistake that he would make, Zack is revealed as the Gormogon's apprentice. Information Zack provides leads to the killer.

Booth's return from the dead is quickly pushed aside when clues from an explosion in the lab lead investigators to suspect that someone at the Jeffersonian is assisting Gormogon. That person presumably switched the ingredients Zack was mixing, which caused the explosion. Dr. Sweets works up a profile suggesting that it could be Hodgins, but Cam suspects the psychologist. Neither would prove to be correct, though the suspicions mirrored the debate that was going on in the audience. The way this plotline played out was also one of the producers' biggest regrets about having to work around the writers' strike.

"It would have been such fun to play it out longer," Hart Hanson laments. "The original plan was to make Hodgins a credible suspect as the Gormogon and make Sweets a credible suspect. And certainly a lot of the online people thought it must be Sweets because he appeared in time for that to happen. It was just happenstance that he appeared: that's the way things work in TV sometimes. But we did everything we could to subtly make them suspects. In 'The Pain in the Heart' I think we were fairly successful at having the fingers pointed everywhere."

John Francis Daley acknowledges the fans certainly believed it was him. "It was

the first real glimpse that I got at the fanbase of the show and how invested the people are in the stories," he admits. "I was reading about all the speculation that I could be the killer, I had no idea that it would become such a big mystery. I would actually be stopped on the street by people saying, 'Are you the Gormogon?' I'd be with my girlfriend sometimes and she had absolutely no idea what they were talking about. I had to explain, 'Yeah, they think I'm a serial killer.'"

TJ Thyne, however, was never in doubt about his character, Jack Hodgins. "We wanted to keep the audience guessing, so of course Jack had to wear the 'looks-guilty' hat for a while, but at the end of the day, it's not Jack. He's not that guy. Never could or would be that guy. He believes too much in the good of people. It's why he *is* a conspiracy theorist, watching how the

world wrongs the right. It's why as a billionaire several times over, he's choosing to spend his days and nights working for Dr. Brennan at the Jeffersonian, always in the hope of solving another puzzle to stop another murderer from walking free. Jack would never admit that to you, of course, he'd tell you he just loves the science, but it's what drives him."

In the end, it is Zack who is revealed as the Gormogon apprentice. He set up the explosion, but it turned out to be larger than he intended because he held off on the experiment to protect Hodgins. The delay altered the mixture enough to make it more volatile. Zack confesses to killing the lobbyist, but admits that he did not eat the man. Caroline Julian cuts a deal to have Zack institutionalized instead of imprisoned, even though Sweets notes that he is clearly mentally acute. This ending didn't

Polymethylmethacrylate: A clear thermoplastic.

'Bad Luck' by Social Distortion, *Greatest Hits*

only surprise the fans, but the actor as well.

Eric Millegan, a devout basketball fan, had been passing his time during the writers' strike by following his beloved Portland Trailblazers on the road. He was in Sacramento towards the end of the strike when he got a call informing him that Hart Hanson and Stephen Nathan wanted to meet with him. Millegan called the showrunner to see what was up, which is when he learned that he was no longer going to be a series regular. Millegan kept the meeting with his producers, and had some very logical questions. He explains, "I went to the meeting and they're like, 'So, Zack's

Zack: You looked at the mandible.

Brennan: You had to know I'd see it eventually.

Zack: I didn't foresee the extent of my injuries. I was going to sneak out of here but...

Brennan: ...your friends never left your side.

assisting the Gormogon.' I was like, 'What? Did he eat people?'" Once he was assured that Zack was not a cannibal, Millegan saw the potential in the story. "It was shocking, but it was also kind of exciting," he admits. "Zack was sort of a victim. I certainly didn't play it that he was evil. He was just misled. Then we found out in season four that he didn't actually kill anyone."

Millegan took the news in his stride, but the same could not be said for the fans. The reaction was swift and it was loud, but one wonders how it would have been if the writers had gone with their initial plan. "The original idea was that Zack would be a

victim of the Gormogon and not his apprentice," Hart Hanson admits. "But we just didn't want to end on that note. We actually thought we could bring Zack back for more episodes and he could get some more money. I should have been harsher and meaner and crueler. We will be next time." He adds that last part with a laugh that, hopefully, suggests he's joking about the possibility of losing another character.

The change was not just hard for Millegan and the fans, but for his family of cast mates as well. His friends in the cast would continue to keep in touch and hang out with him outside of work, but they wouldn't have him around every day. "Personally, it was pretty hard for everybody," Michaela Conlin comments, echoing the sentiments of every cast member. "Eric and TJ and I had all been the original Squints in the beginning, starting the show at the pilot. That was a strange adjustment. Not to mention that he's friends with all of us personally. It was hard. It was very emotional. In shooting his last episode, nobody really had to act. It was all very sad, because we all knew it was coming and we all shot the stuff in the hospital together. He's a total sweetheart. I miss him, but I do get to see him. I think that he has left an indelible mark on the show."

"It was a shocker for both Bones and me," Emily Deschanel adds. "Zack worked for a serial killer? Gormogon! I think everyone was surprised by that. No one would expect that from Zack. Sure, Zack is socially awkward, and logical to a fault, but I don't think anyone dreamed he would kill someone! And it turns out he didn't. But Brennan doesn't know that. An evil man took advantage of someone by using his weak spot. Emily misses Zack and Eric and so does Brennan."

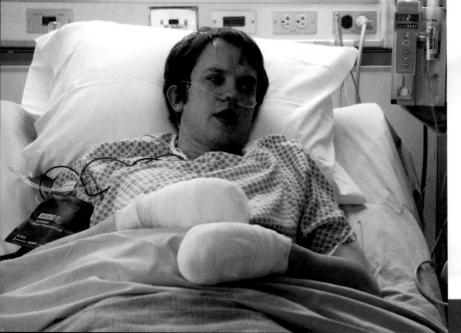

THE THIGH BONE'S CONNECTED TO THE BACKBONE...
INTO SEASON FOUR

Production on the fourth season of *Bones* began while the third season was still wrapping after the writers' strike. Extra episodes that were filmed during the spring of 2008 were held until fall, meaning that the new season would have an impressive twenty-six episodes to make up for the shortened previous season.

Following a typical summer hiatus, the production continued filming season four with 'The Perfect Pieces in the Purple Pond' and the brief return of Zack Addy. *Bones* continued to grow both in the ratings and critical acclaim, and with their success came the problem of having to come up with more stories and, more importantly, reasons to keep the two main characters apart romantically even though everyone wants to see them get together.

> **Booth:** *I'm not saying that we should have a king, or a queen, or beheadings, and all that jazz. I'm just saying, you know, calling someone "Sir Seeley Booth," now that is civilized.*
>
> **Brennan:** *What makes you think that you would be knighted?*
>
> **Booth:** *Come on, you're serious right? Please.*

While mysteries provide the framework for the show, the writers know they are not the only thing that brings people back week after week. "I think we have people who love mysteries," executive producer Stephen Nathan acknowledges, "but we also have a very, very large segment of our audience that tunes in specifically for the characters. I think that's always what makes a show endure. You can talk about classics like *ER* and *L.A. Law*. You're very hard-pressed to remember specific cases, but you certainly remember the characters and the relationships they were having. I think that's what we go for here. What sustains the show is good, solid mysteries, because that's the foundation of the show. If those are solid, then it lets us do all this extra character work."

This, naturally, brings the writers to the challenge of keeping those relationships fresh week in and week out. As Hart Hanson notes, "The main thing is to change the relationships amongst our leads, particularly Brennan and Booth, without removing the story engine; without removing the things that make them enjoyable to watch. The main manifestation of that is their romantic chemistry. But it's also the way they each approach the world that gives us a take on each case. We have to make sure that matures and develops organically but does not change so radically that we eviscerate the difference between them that give us our series."

With that challenge in mind for the fourth season, the producers stayed true to the core of the show, while shaking things up in new and interesting ways. Rather than hiring someone to fill the void left by Zack, instead, a series of rotating interns, each with their own personality quirks, would attempt to replace the irreplaceable. Hodgins and Angela would break up in a manner that, even

> *Brennan: If any kind of people could murder someone and get away with it, it would be us.*

the producers admit, both characters had the power to stop. Sweets would write his book on Booth and Brennan while providing profiling techniques for the cases. And Cam would reveal a very telling part of her past and take on a new challenge as a mom.

Booth and Brennan continue their frustrating, flirtatious dance, both in the U.S. and abroad. Moving the show "across the pond" for a pair of episodes was another benefit of the growing success of the series. "It's one of the reasons we started season four in England," claims executive producer Barry Josephson. "We knew how popular we were there. I have traveled all over the world and seen the show. I've seen it in New Zealand and in Australia. I've seen it in France and England. I saw it in Tahiti, which was fun. I got to see it in French twice. It's remarkable. It's great to talk to people who are fans of the show there and see that it really does translate. I think we're now shown in almost 200 countries. We have fans all over."

SEASON FOUR

Regular cast:

David Boreanaz: *Special Agent Seeley Booth*

Emily Deschanel: *Dr. Temperance Brennan*

Michaela Conlin: *Angela Montenegro*

Tamara Taylor: *Dr. Camille Saroyan*

TJ Thyne: *Dr. Jack Hodgins*

John Francis Daley: *Dr. Lance Sweets*

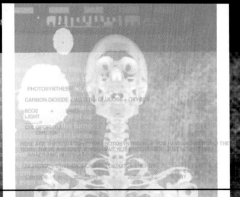

YANKS IN THE U.K. PART ONE

WRITTEN BY HART HANSON & KARINE ROSENTHAL
DIRECTED BY IAN TOYNTON

GUEST STARRING: EUGENE BYRD (DR. CLARK EDISON), SEAN BLAKEMORE (GRAYSON BARASA), MICHAEL BRANDON (ROGER FRAMPTON), ANDREW BUCHAN (DR. IAN WEXLER), TUPPENCE MIDDLETON (VERA WATERHOUSE), ED COLEMAN (CYRIL BIBBY), TY GLASER (HEATHER MILLER), BEN RIGHTON (HARRY BONHAM), DAVID YELLAND (DUKE GERALS BONHAM), JANE HOW (ANNE BONHAM), SHEILA REID (PAIGE BONHAM), INDIRA VARMA (INSPECTOR CATE PRITCHARD)

- The body of wealthy American socialite Portia Frampton is found, along with her car, in the River Thames. Being that the victim is American with a wealthy father, Inspector Cate Pritchard of Scotland Yard invites Booth and Brennan to assist as they are in England on business.
- The victim has a penetrating trauma to the parietal bone. Trauma to the **zygomatic bone** suggests that she fell to the ground and was struck repeatedly. Microscopic traces of mother-of-pearl are found in the skull fragments.
- The victim was dating the heir to the Duke of Innesford. Fatty acid composition of the victim's cervical fluid suggests that she was pregnant.
- It is determined that the victim suffered from Von-Hippel Lindau disease, a hereditary illness that neither of her parents seemed to have, but both the Duke and his mother show signs of. The Duke confesses that Portia had come to him questioning him about her parentage.
- Crushed scleractinian coral and organic material from an antique rose bush are found in the treads of the vehicle's tires. Brennan finds similar materials in the tires of their rental car, suggesting that the substance came from the private road of the Bonham Estate. A mother of pearl fireplace poker found in the Duke's home appears to be the murder weapon. The butler admits to the killing.

The idea for filming in England grew out of a fortuitous misunderstanding on the part of Hart Hanson. Consulting producer Josh Berman, who used to work on *CSI*, had told Hanson of a plan for his former show to journey to England for an episode. "What I heard him say," Hanson reveals, "was that *CSI* had convinced their English broadcaster to foot the bill for an episode to shoot in England, and I thought, 'What a great idea. Booth and Bones in England.' Of course, it hadn't happened with *CSI* and it didn't happen with us," Hanson explains. "Our English broadcaster was not going to pony up that money. But we did find that if we only took David and Emily, our director of photography, Gordon Lonsdale, our director, Ian Toynton, and me; if we took just us and got a small efficient crew in England and shot a two-parter, then we could probably swing it financially."

The producers were able to use those financial constraints creatively, as Stephen Nathan explains: "We found out how much money we had, where we could shoot, and then backed our stories up into those parameters. It could not have come out better."

The actors also appreciated the change of scene. "It was completely different to film in England," Emily Deschanel notes. "First of all, our crew was about half the size it usually is, and everyone does different jobs over there." But the biggest, and most welcome difference had to be the public reaction in the U.K. "People would gather around to watch us film," she says. "No one cares in L.A., people don't gather around to watch us. I guess we have a lot of fans over there."

Back in the States, Angela's husband arrives on the scene leading Hodgins and Angela to a deeper examination of their relationship. "I like to think this is how we

Booth: Me 'n Bones, we are the greatest crime-solving team in America.

Brennan: But this is England.

do everything on *Bones*," Hart Hanson says. "It's what we get criticized for and praised for; which is that thing of fulfilling the audience's expectations in a way they don't expect. The typical story would be that the perfect man shows up and ruins their relationship. We didn't quite do it that way. It did happen, but it doesn't happen in the way you would expect, which is Angela runs off with him. Something about him showing up ruined things between Hodgins and Angela and broke them up for the time being."

Eventually Barasa realizes that Angela is meant to be with Hodgins, thanks to a little cosmic intervention. Hanson explains, "I knew that we had to have the moment in part one where we tell the audience these two are made to be together forever and they will never break up," Hanson explains. "Then the question is, what is the re-creation of the bell? You didn't want church bells going off—that's what happened between Angela and Barasa. You didn't want a truck of bells going by. You wanted something special.

"Coincidentally, my oldest son, Ben, rides with a group of cyclists who do these midnight rides through L.A. They ride in a huge mass, wearing costumes. It's a wild, traveling carnival. And I thought, 'Ah, that's what's going to happen. Those people are going to drive by all ringing their bells.'" The producers cast a group of extras to ride through the Fox backlot and added Hanson's son and some of his friends in the mob ringing their bells. "It was actually magic enough on the street in the moment that we knew it would work," recalls Hanson. "Ian Toynton, was so delighted when it happened. It was sur-real. It was weird. But it seemed to work."

Zygomatic bone: Cheekbone.

'Raise Today' by Peasant, *On the Ground*

YANKS IN THE U.K. PART TWO

WRITTEN BY STEPHEN NATHAN & SCOTT WILLIAMS
DIRECTED BY IAN TOYNTON

GUEST STARRING: EUGENE BYRD (DR. CLARK EDISON), SEAN BLAKEMORE (GRAYSON BARASA), MICHAEL BRANDON (ROGER FRAMPTON), ANDREW BUCHAN (DR. IAN WEXLER), TUPPENCE MIDDLETON (VERA WATERHOUSE), ED COLEMAN (CYRIL BIBBY), JONATHAN WRATHER (EMERSON), ROCKY MARSHALL (LAKE), DAVID FAHM (PALMER), INDIRA VARMA (INSPECTOR CATE PRITCHARD)

- Booth and Brennan are called to the burned apartment of Dr. Ian Wexler to examine the remains of his charred body.
- Wexler signed a writ of release shortly before his death certifying that the Roger Frampton's construction site had no historical importance. Checks made out to Wexler from a shell corporation owned by Frampton are later found—he was bribing Wexler to close his dig.
- A shattered section of femur from another body matches up with the stab wounds on the victim's body, suggesting that it was the murder weapon.
- The bone displays high levels of **mercury fulminate** and has been **ossified**, indicating that it is over two thousand years old. Conjecturing that the bone could have been found at the construction site, it would have stopped Frampton from developing the property.
- The mercury fulminate is traced back to the soil in a section of dig overseen by Wexler's student, Vera Waterhouse. As the bone has no hilt, the suspect would have scraped her hand when she stabbed Wexler. Waterhouse has a matching wound on her hand and admits that Wexler wanted to return the bribe money the two of them had taken from Frampton when they found out the truth about the site: it *did* have historical value. Vera was afraid her career would be ruined if it was revealed she had accepted a bribe.

The second part of the 'Yanks in the U.K.' two-hour season opener continued to use the foreign setting as a way of opening up the characters to new experiences. It was a technical challenge to coordinate an episode where the Booth and Brennan scenes were shot in one time zone and the Squints' scenes in another. "We filmed all of the U.S. parts here on our sets first," explains producer Jan DeWitt. "After that our key players traveled to London to shoot the rest of the episode. It was definitely a challenge, especially for Ian Toynton,

who had to juggle two episodes at the same time."

It certainly helped that Toynton was working in his homeland. "What a position to be in that your producer/ director is British," notes Steve Beers. "Ian has spent a good portion of his career over there. He knows how it all works, and who the really good people to work with are. We worked with some very talented producers."

The stateside subplot in both episodes revolves around the end of the Angela/ Hodgins relationship, something that few people saw coming.

"I think she was beginning to feel kept by him and by that situation," Michaela Conlin says, of the breakup. "I think she wants to be with somebody who makes her feel the opposite. I don't know whether that's going to be him; I certainly hope so. There's part of me that some days just wants to slap her and say, 'You're in love with him! Just get it over with! What's with the two of you?' I think that they both need to grow up a little bit, honestly, and figure out how they're going to love each other."

Angela: My heart isn't yours to claim. It's mine to give away.

TJ Thyne asserts, "Angela Montenegro is and always will be the love of Jack's life. She's the one that got away. He's learned, over the years, that it's her way or no way. When it comes to day-to-day decisions in their relationship that's fine. He's cool with her winning every argument—which you know she does," he laughs. "But when it comes to his own heart; when it comes to her constantly walking away from him and wanting her own freedom... well... there is only so much he, or any man, can take before wondering, 'Wait a minute... am I *not* the one she wants?'"

But is it really the end? There was that moment with the bells....

"The universe has spoken," Hart Hanson reassures us all. "These two are meant to be together. I always maintained that if an adult had been sitting with them during their breakup, that adult would have said, 'Stop it. You're falling off a wall here that you don't have to fall off.' We will return to that theme someday; we will go back and see what happened there. I certainly got varying responses on the breakup scene. Some people said it made no sense; others seemed to get what happened to them. Either one of them could have stopped what happened from happening if they'd wanted to. I believe that they belong together. I think we want them together. The actors want them to be together. The characters want to be together. And so does the audience. Who would be stupid enough to resist all that?"

Mercury fulminate: A gray, crystalline solid used in tanneries and for the manufacture of explosives.
Ossified: Hardened by deposits of mineral matter.

'Fool for U' by Plantlife, *Time Traveler*
'Ghost of a Chance' by Ron Sexsmith, *Exit Strategy of the Soul*

THE MAN IN THE OUTHOUSE

TELEPLAY BY CARLA KETTNER   STORY BY MARK LISSON
DIRECTED BY STEVEN DEPAUL

GUEST STARRING: CARLA GALLO (DAISY WICK), SCOOT MCNAIRY (NOEL LIFTIN), LISA LACKEY (VERONICA LANDAU), JILL WAGNER (HOLLY MARKWELL), TIM GRIFFIN (PETE STECKEL), MICHELE GREENE (AMANDA O'ROURKE), ROB BOLTIN (JASON DEFRY), BRENNAN ELLIOTT (MARK GAFFNEY), RICHARD GANT (ARTHUR LANG), JOHN DIMAGGIO (JIM DODD), DEE FREEMAN (SGT. FRANCIS DIAMOND)

- A man's remains are found under an outhouse that exploded from high methane levels. The victim has a gunshot wound to the frontal lobe, and a composite suggests that it is Bill O'Roarke, host of *Busted By Bill*, a show about cheating spouses.
- Remnants of a photograph are found lodged in the victim's throat. Angela is able to reconstruct enough of the image to see that it is a picture of a couple having sex, and the woman in the photo has a tattoo.
- Hairline fractures at the base of the victim's skull contain particles of chlorinated polyethylene, a rubber used on the tail of a microphone.
- A swab of the victim's inner thigh reveals a trace of enamel iron and a fleck of silver plating. There was also the presence of saliva with **candidiasis**, suggesting that a person with an infected tongue piercing had been with the victim. Holly Markwell, a staff member on the show, has such a tongue piercing and a tattoo that matches the one in the photo.
- The photo is determined to be a print from an email attachment, which is tracked back to Markwell's boyfriend, Pete Steckel, a cameraman on the show. Steckel admits that the photo came from the victim's wife, Amanda O'Roarke. She admits to sending the photo, but claims that it wasn't her intention for her husband to be killed. She cannot be charged since she was not directly involved in his death.

Booth discovers that Brennan is dating two men: a blue-collar worker named Mark and a botanist named Jason. Though she sees no problem in conducting two relationships that exist for separate reasons, Booth has his concerns with the set up. Brennan quickly learns he isn't the only one when she accidentally makes two dates for the same time and winds up losing both men.

Following the departure of Clark Edison in the previous episode, Brennan begins to interview other possible replacements for Zack out of a pool of her best interns. She begins the search with Daisy Wick, who

has a difficult time fitting in, largely due to her overeager approach to her work.

The first episode back from London opens with a bang in the bucolic setting of an outhouse by an empty road. It's not a standout location, by any means, but it was another example of the continuing challenges that face the production team in almost every episode. The series is set in the Washington D.C. area and the characters often travel around the country. Since the production is filmed almost exclusively on the West Coast in L.A., the production staff have to find ways to give the show an East Coast feel.

Location managers Deborah Laub and Stephen Weissberger alternate their location scouting duties with Laub taking the odd numbered episodes and Weissberger working on the even. As with everything on the show, their work begins with the script. Deborah Laub describes the process: "We read the script and make a list of the locations indicated. We start gathering any information we need from the internet and our personal and show picture files. We try to have as many options for locations that we can gather to

Booth: Being faithful is what separates us from chimps.

Brennan: Actually, it's a gene called HAR1F.

present to the production designer, episode director, and producers directly after the concept meeting."

The concept meeting is where the writers, producers and the director set out their vision of the script to the various department heads so they can discuss the prop, costume, special effects, and other needs for the particular episode. The location managers come armed with their choices for places outside the studio to shoot, but that is only the beginning of the process. "After the meeting we all usually look at some pictures of location possibilities," Stephen Weissberger explains. "And then we head out in a van to see those locations in person."

Considering that the majority of their locations are supposed to be on the East Coast, filming in Los Angeles has an upside and a downside. "Trying to avoid palm trees and Mediterranean style architecture can sometimes prove challenging," Weissberger notes. While Laub agrees, she does add that, "Los Angeles has all types of architecture, so it's not difficult to find most styles for either residential or commercial locations. L.A. has an amazingly diverse landscape: we have oceans, deserts, and mountains, all within a short driving distance. We have managed to find areas to work for the Chesapeake Bay, deciduous forests, green pastureland, East Coast highways, marshland and many, many green vistas. With its diverse landscape, various architectural styles and great weather, I don't think L.A. can be beat for location filming."

Candidiasis: A thrush infection.

'I Hurt Too' by Katie Herzig, *Apple Tree*

THE FINGER IN THE NEST

WRITTEN BY LYLA OLIVER   DIRECTED BY JEFF WOOLNOUGH

GUEST STARRING: CESAR MILLAN (HIMSELF), DEAN NORRIS (DON TIMMONS), DEVON GRAYE (ROBBIE TIMMONS), ADAM ROSE (DR. ANDREW HOPP), SUSAN CHUANG (KAREN LANDREW), HEIDI SWEDBERG (ALICE ELLIOT), DEMETRIUS GROSSE (TUCKER PAYNE), MICHAEL BADALUCCO (SCOTT STARRET)

- A finger in a bird's nest has a jagged appearance where it was severed from the hand of a body located eight miles away. Lividity indicates that the victim died elsewhere and was dumped. Missing person Dr. Seth Elliot matches the victim's description.
- Deep puncture wounds to the trachea pierced the jugular, leading the victim to bleed to death. Saliva found on him, combined with pre-mortem bite marks, suggest that a large domestic dog with filed teeth and a pronounced crack in its canine tooth killed the man.
- Blood is found in Elliot's vehicle along with a prescription bottle belonging to the veterinarian's assistant, Robbie Timmons. Robbie claims he was with his tutor, a third-year medical student named Andrew Hopp, at the time of the murder.
- Video of a dogfight on the victim's PDA is time stamped the day of the murder. A pit full of dog remains is found on Timmons' property, along with a fighting ring and a dozen chained dogs. One of those dogs provides a match for the teeth impression on the victim.
- A review of dog photos reveals a familiar stitch used in sewing the wound of one of the animals. Brennan recognizes it as a match for a practice stitch she saw in Andrew Hopp's possession. Dr. Elliot was planning to turn photos of a dog fight over to the police, but Hopp instructed his dog, Ripley, to kill him first.

During the investigation Brennan bonds with Ripley, the dog that was horribly used to commit a murder. She intends to adopt the victimized animal, but he is put down before she can. Unhappy with the cruel resolution to the crime, she and Booth bury the dog's remains by a lake, after Booth steals him from the morgue.

Everyone on the crew enjoys working with animals, and they are very sensitive to the needs of their furry guest actors. Steve Beers explains, "You get a lot of help from American Humane and use your own kind of sensitivity, but the real challenge is you've got these creatures that don't have a choice about being there, so you have to respect what you ask of them and how you treat them. It's the same as with a young child: they really don't get a choice in this.

"I think the biggest challenge is maintaining a calm environment and knowing what they can do and doing it in such a way that you really aren't affecting the safety and comfort of the animal. Good trainers train their animals through positive reinforcement, whether it's food, love, whatever. The animals that are successful for them within the species that they're dealing with are the animals that have the strongest desire to please a person. That's why dogs are so great. You can train a dog to food, but what a dog wants more than anything is to please you. If you have an environment where it

Brennan: Ripley was a good dog. He didn't want to fight but he did it to please his master. He didn't want to attack a human being but he did it to please his master. It wasn't Ripley's fault that his master was cruel and selfish. Like all dogs, Ripley only saw the good in people. Dogs are like that. People should take a lesson.

works that way with animals, it's great."

The environment within the Jeffersonian is a little less hospitable towards Brennan's latest grad student, who is working on the case as well as Hodgins's last nerve. The older student once sold Hodgins a car that broke down, but the anger Hodgins has been expressing lately has more to do with other factors than an old lemon. Sweets eventually gets Hodgins to admit where his anger stems from.

"Jack was fighting with everyone," TJ Thyne explains. "He had major symptoms heading toward depression. Cam and Brennan were having to snap him back into it. He was yelling at the interns.

Then, finally, one day, when Michael Badalucco was guest starring as one of Brennan's interns, Jack broke. He started opening up, admitting how lost he felt without Angela, and without Zack. He literally found himself sitting across from Sweets in his office. We all know Jack and Brennan think psychology is a soft science, thus a pointless one. And yet, there Jack was on Sweets' couch, opening up. When Sweets says that it's normal and fine that Jack's behaving the way he is, then... well... it made Jack realize he wasn't crazy. He wasn't losing it. Slowly, he began his climb back to being the Jack we love—the true king of the lab—which is where we find him for the rest of season four."

THE PERFECT PIECES IN THE PURPLE POND

WRITTEN BY JOSH BERMAN   DIRECTED BY JEANNOT SZWARC

- Twelve body parts, not including the head, are found in an evaporation pool in an industrial area. A slight spinal curvature, hypermobile joints, and collagen deficiency suggest the victim had **Ehlers-Danlos syndrome**. Special order children's shoes in an adult size eleven and medical records match a Jared Addison, age twenty-five.

- Hesitation marks at the point the head was severed from the body suggest that the killer had an emotional connection to the victim.

- Upon reviewing the victim's childlike and well-ordered bedroom, Sweets determines that the victim was obsessive-compulsive, agoraphobic, and had classic Peter Pan syndrome. A photo of an older woman is found in the room along with a phone number.

- The victim's girlfriend informs investigators that Addison was attending a behavior modification conference to cure his OCD and other issues so he could move out of his mother's home.

- Considering that everything in the victim's home is ordered in groupings of twelve—just like his body—this points to the killer also having OCD and access to Addison's bedroom, suggesting it was the victim's mother. It is believed that she murdered her son because he was attempting to cure himself of his issues and pull away from her. She buried her son's head in the backyard.

Dr. Sweets is frustrated by his interviews with an institutionalized Zack Addy who claims to feel no remorse over his involvement with the Gormogon killer. A later visit from Hodgins is almost as uncomfortable, but the friends bond over a case and Hodgins leaves the file behind for Zack to work on. Of course, no one expected him to break out of the institution to offer his help with the investigation. But the bigger surprise comes when Dr. Sweets returns him to the institution and Zack admits to his therapist that he never committed murder; he just told the Gormogon where to find his victim. Zack insists that he would have killed the man if The Master had instructed him to, but Sweets challenges that belief. Either way, Zack refuses to let the truth be known because, as an accessory to murder, he feels he would be taken out of the sanitarium and placed in prison.

It was the episode fans of Eric Millegan (both in the audience and in the cast and crew) were waiting for: the return of Zack Addy. It came relatively early in the season; in fact, it came particularly early into the filming of season four. Since Fox had tacked the production of a few season

Brennan: I don't want to be a sexy scientist.

Booth: Well, that's like me saying I don't want to be a sexy F.B.I. Agent. We can't change who we are.

four episodes onto the end of the post-strike filming in season three, 'The Perfect Pieces in the Purple Pond' was actually the first episode to be filmed after the usual hiatus.

For Eric Millegan, it was like coming back from summer vacation along with everybody else. "It felt like I hadn't even been gone much yet when I went in," the actor says. "I just felt like I didn't do any scenes in those other episodes. I hadn't really felt like I had left yet." Still, Millegan admits it was great to be among friends again. "The cast is so great to work with. It was fun reconnecting with everyone. I still hang out with all the people off the set, too. Emily and I went out a few weeks ago.

Tamara and Michaela and I are supposed to get together soon. I still see everybody."

Zack would return in the season finale as well, but those visits didn't stop his friends onset—both the characters and the actors —from missing him. "Cam and Zack got close," Tamara Taylor says. "I think she really, really cares for Zack. When she found out [he was working with Gormogon], I think it was the furthest thing from her mind and the biggest disappointment. I absolutely love Eric Millegan. He's still around, and they didn't replace him. But, for selfish reasons, I loved coming into work every day and playing with him."

Ehlers-Danlos syndrome: A rare genetic disorder of the connective tissue caused by a defect in collagen synthesis.

'Set Free' by Katie Gray, *From Far Away*

THE CRANK IN THE SHAFT

WRITTEN BY *ELIZABETH BENJAMIN*   DIRECTED BY *STEVEN DEPAUL*

GUEST STARRING: JOEL DAVID MOORE (COLIN FISHER), EWAN CHUNG (CHIP YAP), KATHARINE LEONARD (CHRISTINE GERTIN), PETE GARDNER (GARY FLANNERY), DEVIN MCGINN (TED RUSSO), KIM ROBILLARD (DAVE FARFIELD), EDWARD JAMES GAGE (STAN NOKES)

• A woman's remains are found smeared along the elevator shaft of an office building. The absence of hemorrhagic tissue suggests the victim was dead before she was dropped into the shaft. A sketch of the victim matches the I.D. photo of missing office manager Patty Hoyle.

• Bilateral compression fractures on ribs R3 to R11 are found with an inward deformation on the lateral aspects. Curved patterns are consistent with the outer edge of a shoe, suggesting the victim was stomped on both sides of her ribcage. Semen stains are also found on the victim's skirt and in a swatch of carpet from the copy room.

• A dark stain in the **squamous bone** consistent with blunt force trauma lacks staining on the exterior of the bone, suggesting that the stain was caused by a ruptured aneurysm. Two tiny punctures in the skull suggest that a staple had cause the puncture, rupturing the aneurysm. A small depression near the wound indicates that the stapler was thrown at the victim.

• DNA sequences in the semen sample reveal that it came from a person of Asian descent, suggesting it belongs to office worker Chip Yap. A piece of fingernail with blue polish is found on the grooves of the elevator door, matching polish worn by the receptionist, Christine Gertin. Gertin admits to throwing the stapler when the victim found her and Yap making love in the copy room and was going to report them.

In the wake of a coworker's death, Booth is not mourning the man so much as he is covetous of his office chair. And he's not the only one. It is apparently the most sought after chair in the F.B.I. Booth asks both Brennan and Cam for doctors' letters providing a medical reason for why he needs the chair. Brennan refuses to lie for him, but she does give human resources a call to remind them of her partner's worth and how he deserves the chair. Booth gets the sought after item only to find that it is not as comfortable as he thought.

In an episode rife with inter-office politics, set decorator Kimberly Wannop found herself with a relatively unusual situation compared to her usual *Bones* assignments. The setting for much of 'The Crank in the Shaft' is not in some dark and dingy underground labyrinth. It does not take place in a carnival or circus. It is certainly not the Gomorgon vault. The setting for the episode was merely a typical office space. But that does not mean that Wannop couldn't approach it with an artistic eye. "We had an entire vacant office to work with," she explains. "Michael Mayer [production designer] and I wanted to convey the dullness of the job: no artwork, no pops of color in their world. There was some color art in the lobby but past the point where the cubicles were I made it very boring. The characters were bored with their jobs. We never really know what the company sells or what everyone does. It was key to keep the dressing generic so that it becomes more relatable to the viewers."

In the atypical offices of the Jeffersonian, Angela and Hodgins are having difficulty negotiating their new working relationship in light of the end of their romance. Angela turns to Sweets

Brennan: ...I am a completely independent contractor operating out of the Jeffersonian. In the hive I would be the queen bee.

Booth: You're still in a hive.

Brennan: In which I am queen.

for advice. The young psychologist suggests she undergo therapy with him to explore her feelings, but just talking it out helps her enough to clear the air so she and Hodgins can move on.

The pairing known among fandom as 'Hodgela' moves further apart in this episode. Angela and Hodgins have always been an unusual couple, but their path together has given them the chance to experience the many different sides of a relationship. It's a ride that the producers say serves a larger purpose for the show. "Angela and Hodgins go through things

that the audience kind of wants Booth and Brennan to go through," Stephen Nathan explains. "But their relationship, while it seems fated, is also too complicated for them to figure out quickly. They're upfront about their feelings for each other, but working it out is much more complicated. Angela is somebody who never thought she would commit to one person and is used to going from relationship to relationship; while Hodgins is more of a one girl guy. We're still playing with that relationship. We're not done with them."

Squamous bone: The anterior superior portion of the temporal bone.

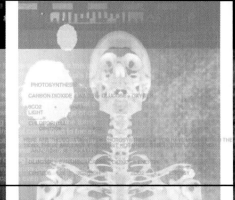

THE HE IN THE SHE

WRITTEN BY KARINA CSOLTY   DIRECTED BY CRAIG ROSS, JR.

- The top half of a skeleton with a cleanly severed spine washes ashore. The victim's fingers show evidence of multiple blows, suggesting foul play. A breast implant contains a serial number traced to missing pastor Patricia Ludmuller.
- A message on the victim's answering machine leads investigators to J.P. Gratton, a married member of the pastor's flock.
- The bottom part of the body is found in the water eight miles from the initial site. The male pelvic bone combined with a vagina indicates that the victim is transgender.
- A composite of Patricia Ludmuller as she might have appeared as a man is instantly recognizable as Patrick Stephenson, a popular television pastor who disappeared six years earlier.
- Fiberglass and resin particulates are found in both the skull wound and the pelvis. The splinters are angled in different directions, suggesting a scenario in which a boat struck the victim twice.
- Based on size, wood-grain, and shape of the keel, the search is narrowed to two models of boat.
- The suspect, J.P. Gratton, owns such a boat with damage where the victim would have grasped onto the side. The seat, which is not adjustable, would only fit the suspect's wife, proving her to be the killer.

GUEST STARRING: RYAN CARTWRIGHT (VINCENT NIGEL-MURRAY), DAVID GALLAGHER (RYAN STEPHENSON), BRUCE THOMAS (J.P. GRATTON), BLAKE SHIELDS (CHUCK KENNEDY), NANCY YOUNGBLUT (CECILIA STEPHENSON), JOHN LIVINGSTON (WADE SCHMIDT), SYLVA KELEGIAN (RITA GRATTON), BRETT GILBERT (HIPPIE #1), DUSTIN HESS (HIPPIE #2)

Brennan and Booth investigate the murder of a pastor in a small seaside town on the East Coast, once again requiring the production to find an L.A. location for a town thousands of miles away. Location manager Stephen Weissberger found that the town of San Pedro came closest to meeting the production's needs. He explains, "Being an old fishing community, San Pedro has a character that is evocative of the East Coast."

'The He in the She' is one of those episodes that cuts right to the heart of the dynamic between Booth and Brennan. Almost every episode gives the writers the chance to explore their main characters' differing views on life. That is no more evident than in the episodes where the writers take on larger issues

exploring life outside of the mainstream. Episodes like 'Death in the Saddle' and 'Mayhem on a Cross' explore diverse subcultures ranging from fetishists, circus folk, and heavy metal enthusiasts. While an episode like 'The He in the She' takes on the serious issues of gender identification and religion, viewing them through the filters of Booth and Brennan.

Stephen Nathan believes that these issue-oriented plot points are very important to the series. "Brennan's a forensic anthropologist," he notes, "she views the world as a scientist in very logical, rational terms. She sees things in anthropological terms. What we see as odd and bizarre, she sees in some sort of historical and sociological context that allows the audience to remove certain

Booth: These peaceful places, there's always a seething underbelly.

Brennan: Really?

Booth: What do I know? I'm from Philly where they put the underbelly on top.

preconceptions that we might hold over very charged issues, like 'The He in the She' or 'Mayhem on a Cross.' It also allows Booth, who seems kind of like Everyman, to confront these situations as well.

"What I like about doing that is we're surprised by the characters. For instance, even with Angela going out with Roxie, she assumed, as the audience did, that Booth would have some sort of issue with that. What we found out was that Booth has an aunt who has a girlfriend. He is crazy about them and he has no problem whatsoever. It's just another way to get us

into the heads of the characters a little bit more and for Brennan to explain certain things to us from a historical anthropological perspective that we wouldn't know. It's very interesting for me as a writer to see the world in that way."

Brennan's latest intern, Mr. Vincent Nigel-Murray, also views the world differently, sharing trivial facts borne from the minutia of everyday life. His tangents often lead to confusion causing him to realize that the straightforward processes of the Jeffersonian staff are not for him... though he will be back.

'River of Sorrow' by Antony & The Johnsons, *Antony & The Johnsons*
'Share' by Bag of Toys, *Nooner*

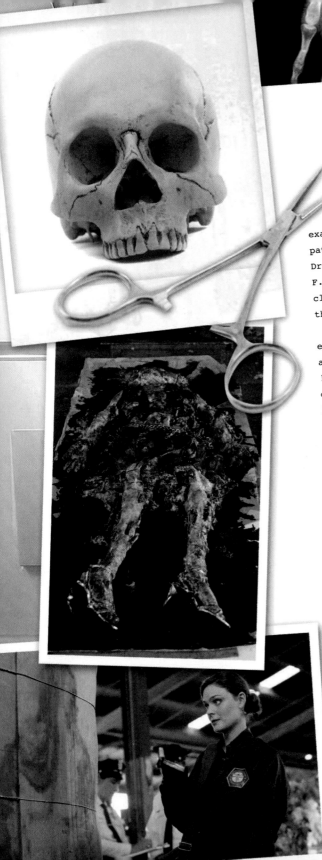

Flesh vs. Bone

The Jeffersonian Medico-Legal Laboratory is staffed with experts in a variety of fields related to the examination of human remains. Under the guidance of pathologist Dr. Camille Saroyan and forensic anthropologist Dr. Temperance Brennan, the staff has cracked some of the F.B.I.'s most challenging murder cases. The two doctors work closely together as experts in their chosen fields, though their areas of expertise are often at odds with one another.

The Jeffersonian gained a reputation for excellence in the examination of skeletal remains when Dr. Brennan accepted a position in the institute. Dr. Saroyan's talents, however, lie in the examination of the flesh, organs, and other soft tissue. At times, this causes the pair of learned doctors to be at loggerheads because a thorough examination of the skeleton cannot be conducted until the soft tissue is removed.

Nowhere was it more evident that the joint examination of flesh and bone can reveal very important clues than in the case of murdered Patricia Ludmuller ('The He in the She'). Skeletal differences between a man and woman are relatively few. Males typically have a narrower pelvic bone, while the female pelvis is shallower and wider to allow for childbirth. It was the appearance of the pelvic bone in the body of Patricia Ludmuller that, combined with a vagina and evidence of breast implants, led investigators to realize that the victim was a post-operative transsexual.

Other areas in the skeletal structure investigators use to determine gender include: the skull, femur, and teeth. Conversely, there are a wealth of differences between the bodies of men and women that can be determined through an examination of the skin, internal organs, and simple visual examination.

As stated earlier, a full examination of the skeleton can only begin once the flesh and organs are removed. Certainly, some evidence can be gathered while the exterior body remains, but a complete cataloguing of the bones is impossible until they are stripped clean. This has, at times, led to conflict in the lab when Dr. Brennan and her staff have been made to wait while Dr.

Saroyan completes her examination.

In the case of deceased student Ashley Clark ('The Salt in the Wounds'), the delay in removing the soft tissue led to the discovery of an important clue. Unable to work directly with the skeleton, Dr. Brennan's intern took a full body X-ray of the bones, piecing them together as a virtual skeleton using borrowed monitors. This allowed for a closer examination of the bones, revealing a hairline fracture in the stapes of the inner ear indicating that it was a murder. Similarly, in the case of deceased bride-to-be

Meriel Mitsakos ('The Cinderella in the Cardboard'), examination through a fluoroscopy machine located a foreign object in the anterior superior iliac spine that otherwise might have been missed.

Dr. Saroyan and Dr. Brennan may place different levels of importance on the usefulness of flesh versus bone in their jobs, but by working together they use their expertise in these different areas to solve numerous crimes.

THE SKULL IN THE SCULPTURE

WRITTEN BY *JANET LIN*   DIRECTED BY *ALLAN KROEKER*

GUEST STARRING: PATRICIA BELCHER (CAROLINE JULIAN), CARLA GALLO (DAISY WICK), VICKI LEWIS (HELEN BRIDENBECKER), JONATHAN LAPAGLIA (ANTON DELUCA), TODD BOSLEY (DUANE), BILL PARKS (CHUNKY), NICHOLE HILTZ (ROXIE LYON)

• Human remains are found in the crushed wreckage of a junked car. It was the sixth vehicle delivered to the junkyard from a gallery where an artist specialized in "crushed car artwork." The artist's assistant and the gallery owner identify a distinctive ring on the victim as belonging to the artist, Geoffrey Thorne.

• A digital rendering of the bones recreates the damage incurred during crushing revealing a fracture to the occipital that was not caused by the car being compacted. Once the skull is reconstructed the shape of the wound indicates that the murder weapon is a common fire ax.

• Limestone and silicone oxide on the victim's clothing suggests he was murdered on the floor of the art gallery. Blood stains are found on the gallery floor, under a layer of turpentine. A fire ax at the location was also wiped clean with turpentine, but the handle reveals sodium chloride and odorants present in human sweat. **Eccrine** pH level is seven, indicating that the murderer was a woman.

• Drugs present in the sweat suggest that the murderer was being treated for **chronic myelogenous leukemia**. One of the drugs, busulfan, causes highly visible skin coloration, which is present on the skin of the gallery owner underneath the kabuki makeup she regularly wears. The woman murdered Thorne so that the price of his artwork would rise and she could afford to pay for her treatment.

Angela tells Hodgins that she intends to start dating again when a girlfriend from her past shows up during the investigation. Angela was involved with Roxie Lyon for over a year in college. Roxie would become a recurring character over the next few episodes, ultimately providing the stimulus for Angela to examine her approach to her love life in a way that she was not ready to do immediately following her breakup with Hodgins. It was fortuitous that the writers had already laid the groundwork, having alluded to this relationship previously on the show. "It didn't come out of thin air," Michaela Conlin reminds us. "It had been mentioned, I think, since the first season. I always like it when we get to see these

peoples' pasts. It's revealing when you get to see who somebody was before they are where we are now. I thought that was a really a nice way to introduce Roxie back into Angela's life, with Roxie coming up literally in the middle of her job. Walking right into the lab, Angela had no choice but to deal with it. That's not really what Angela likes doing, I really liked that it made her kind of a mess."

The messiness continues until the couple break up again in 'The Salt in the Wounds.' The brief relationship gave Conlin new levels to explore with her character. "She's always the one that's doling out the love advice," Conlin notes. "It was really nice getting advice from everybody else. She goes to Brennan–she

Caroline: You can still examine it, you just can't disrupt it in any way. Don't worry, this is just temporary; we'll see how artistic everyone feels when it starts stinking. Just don't scratch it.

Cam: Don't scratch the crushed automobile that encases the rotting dead body?

Caroline: Good. We understand each other.

even goes to Booth. I thought it was a really nice reversal in that respect, getting to see her being more vulnerable."

The writers used Roxie as a launching point to take Angela to that next level, but also to help her get back some of the characteristics they felt she had lost along the way. Stephen Nathan explains, "Roxie was kind of an odd way to help Angela deal with getting over all the turmoil with Hodgins. It seemed that we had an organic way to bring her back into the show, and to have Angela revisit a part of her past, which also got us back a little bit to that free spirit, bohemian character that we always wanted Angela to be. It really sparked something in Michaela. She just rose to the occasion. She's really owned that kind of free spirit, fun, eccentric, spontaneous person in the lab. We don't have anybody else in the lab who will say or do anything."

Eccrine: Related to the sweat glands located throughout the skin.
Chronic myelogenous leukemia: An abnormal increase of the myeloid cells in the bone marrow and blood.

'Shiver' by Madita, *Too*
'Happy Ground' by Pete Murray, *Summer at Eureka*

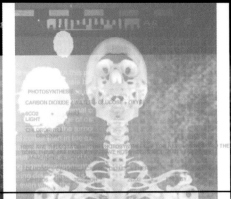

THE CON MAN IN THE METH LAB

WRITTEN BY *KARINE ROTHENTHAL*
DIRECTED BY *ALLISON LIDDI-BROWN*

GUEST STARRING: *EUGENE BYRD (DR. CLARK EDISON), BRIAN HOWE (SHERIFF LEONARD WILKINSON), JOSEPH C. PHILLIPS (COLONEL RYAN WOLCHUCK), MANDY FREUND (LILY STEGMAN), ERIC LADIN (PAUL STEGMAN), ERIC LANGE (STEVE JACKSON), JON WELLNER (MIKE CAMPBELL), CHRISTOPHER GOODMAN (F.B.I. POLICE INSTRUCTOR), BRENDAN FEHR (JARED BOOTH)*

- During a state police training exercise a burning corpse is ejected from an exploding meth lab. The victim had been shot in the chest. Tissue on the right cheek is covered with abrasions in a cross-hatch pattern.
- A series of technical drawings are found in the pocket of the man's windbreaker along with a patent application for a Paul Stegman. Mr. Stegman identifies the victim as his recently reunited father, Jim. Inconsistencies in the description of the man's father later reveal that the victim was misidentified. The victim's DNA is then matched on the felony database to Anthony Pongetti, a man with multiple fraud convictions.
- The remains of the real Jim Stegman are found in the Jeffersonian's bone storage. Bullets found in both victims came from the same gun.
- A large sum of money arrived in the mail at the Stegman home after Pongetti went missing. Some of the cash was bundled in evidence bands from the County Sheriff's Headquarters in Bowie. The stolen money had been confiscated in a drug bust and was supposed to be shipped to the Federal Reserve two weeks earlier.
- It is determined that Sherriff Wilkinson was involved in the theft, suggesting that he killed the victims. The grating in the sheriff's car matches the abrasion pattern on Pongetti's cheek.

'The Con Man in the Meth Lab' opens with a bang when the titular lab explodes during a state police training exercise. This isn't the first time an explosion has rocked the series, but it was one of the standout moments for the crew. "It's hard to choose favorite episodes, since our writers always provide great material," says producer Jan DeWitt. "I can say that episodes that stand out are those with explosions. We've blown up a motor home, an outhouse, the inside of our own lab, and

flipped a taxi. It's very exciting to be present on those days."

While explosions are exciting, they do require a lot of coordination between departments. None of the real planning can begin until the team has found a safe location to blow things up. Location manager Stephen Weissberger details how the first step in any search begins with bureaucracy. "Usually when we get a script that involves special effects, such as explosions or heavy gunfire, I will call both the city's film permit office and the fire department—depending upon the city or area—to make sure they're open to the idea for the location we have in mind. If they're willing to talk and meet with us, that's a very good sign. There are certain cities or jurisdictions that are more difficult than others. Both the County and City of Los Angeles fire departments are very friendly toward our filming needs."

When Booth inexplicably turns over all credit on the high profile mob case to the state troopers, Brennan calls him on it, not realizing that his hand had been forced in order to keep his brother Jared's DUI

Brennan: Your facial structure is even more symmetrical and pleasing than Booth's.

Jared: (to Booth) Is she coming on to me?

Booth: No. It's just the way she talks.

charge under wraps. In the end, she realizes her mistake and apologizes.

With the major crisis in the Brennan family resolved in Max Keenan's acquittal, the writers shifted their focus to Booth's family for more of the drama in season four. Stephen Nathan explains why he feels this family element is crucial to *Bones*. "I think the more people watch the show and follow the characters, the more they want to learn about them. I guess that's kind of a simplistic thing to say, but it's true emotionally. You don't want the characters running in place. We are an episodic show, not a soap opera, but at the same time you want to give loyal fans a rich and full life for every character, and that always requires family. When you learn about their individual families you learn more about how the characters relate to each other. The more they share that with each other, the closer they get, the more vulnerable they are, and specifically with Booth and Brennan, the closer they become. That's obviously what the audience is always looking for with the two of them."

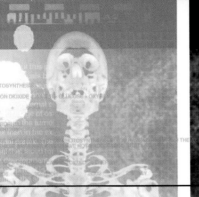

THE PASSENGER IN THE OVEN

WRITTEN BY *CARLA KETTNER*   DIRECTED BY *STEVEN DEPAUL*

GUEST STARRING: PATRICIA BELCHER (CAROLINE JULIAN), PEGGY MILEY (CHARLOTTE UTLEY), AMY FARRINGTON (KATE MCNUTT), WILLIAM R. MOSES (ARTHUR BILBREY), DYLLAN CHRISTOPHER (ELI BILBRY), KEITH DIAMOND (HOWARD KENDELL), JUDSON MILLS (NICK DEVITO), LYDIA LOOK (THERESA MING), CHARLES PARNELL (CAPTAIN BLAKE), NICHOLE HILTZ (ROXIE LYON)

- The burned body of first class passenger Elizabeth Jones is found in a large convection microwave oven in the lower galley of a flight to China.
- Inorganic materials containing tiny metal shards and silicon from a microchip are embedded in the victim's sternum.
- A notch mark on the occipital is identified as the point where the victim was knocked unconscious when she struck a metal latch on a catering cart.
- Hairline fractures weakened the integrity of the cranium, causing it to burst when heated. Pinkish coloration on the burned flesh around the **rectus abdominis** indicates the victim was still alive when placed in the oven.
- Caroline Julian and Dr. Sweets interview the victim's boss who reveals that Jones was having an affair with a married man named Artie. His description matches a first class passenger traveling with his sick wife and teenaged son.
- One of the flight attendants admits to witnessing the murder, but only saw the feet of the victim and her attacker. They were both wearing the slippers that are given out to first class passengers. Brennan jury-rigs an ALS emitter and finds blood on the bottom of the slippers of Artie's son, Eli.
- One of the video games in the boy's game-kit is missing, which is deemed to be enough evidence to swear out a warrant for the teen's arrest.

The clock is ticking for Booth and Brennan when they must solve a crime on a flight to China before the plane touches ground and the F.B.I. loses jurisdiction. The trip reminds Brennan how she keeps being distracted from her first passion, identifying ancient remains, because of all the F.B.I. cases she is called in on. Booth fears she is no longer interested in solving crimes with him, but Brennan reminds him that she was the one who forced him to bring her into the field and make them the partners that they are today.

Much of the action in 'The Passenger in the Oven' is confined to the fuselage of an airplane that in reality, unsurprisingly, never left the ground. And, though much of the tension from the episode comes from the need to solve the case before the plane reaches China, the production was in actual fact not even an hour away from their home stages for filming. The airplane interiors were shot at the Air Hollywood airplane mockup studio in Pacoima. As the name implies, Air Hollywood provides airplane mockups for sets that can be modified to suit the needs of a production for filming.

First assistant director Kent Genzlinger admits that the sets did require some considerable modifications. "We actually did a lot of stuff that they hadn't done before," he states. "Modifying the seats for when Brennan and Booth go up and down, modifying the way it was lit, and also building a galley for when they go downstairs to do the forensics work. That was all Michael Mayer, our production designer, who is just outstanding. They really made the plane look great."

The production even augmented the existing sets by renting and purchasing additional items from an airline graveyard in Palmdale. The biggest challenge came from the addition of the lower galley

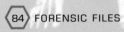

(Brennan is wearing the thick glasses to examine skull pieces as Booth approaches.)

Booth: All right, what I want you to do is take off your glasses, shake out your hair and say, "Mr. Booth, do you know what the penalty is for an overdue book."

Brennan: Why?

Booth: (Disappointed) Never mind.

where the pair conduct their investigation. Steve Beers explains, "It was fun faking it on the set, because the passenger area of the airplane is maybe a foot off the stage floor. We had to fake the actors starting down the stairs and then back onstage build a stairwell that brought them down into the galley. It was fun figuring all that out: how to squeeze it into the inside of a plane mockup that was never designed for that purpose."

Meanwhile, back at the lab, the team's weekend plans are cancelled when the airplane case requires their assistance. Included in those plans is Angela's romantic weekend away with Roxie, which causes Hodgins to question how he feels about Angela moving on. The ensuing discussion between the former lovers prompts Angela to ask Roxie to move in with her—something she's never asked anyone before. Worried that Angela isn't ready for that big of a step, Roxie suggests that they should take it slow.

Rectus abdominis: A paired muscle running vertically along the anterior wall of the abdomen (commonly called the "abs").

'Godspeed' by Jenny Lewis, *Acid Tongue*

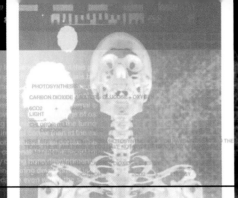

THE BONE THAT BLEW

WRITTEN BY CARLA KETTNER   DIRECTED BY JESSICA LANDAW

- Charred human remains are found in the branches of a tree on government land after presumably being blown there. Traces of an accelerant found on the bones contain **tetraethyl lead**.
- The victim's bone marrow provides a match on the Armed Forces DNA registry to Calvin Warren, a former member of Marine Corps Special Ops, Force Recon. He was in the employ of the King family as the nanny and bodyguard for their children, Lexie and Royce.
- Investigators are led to an area near the King home by tracking surface conditions on the night of a nor'easter with winds strong enough to carry the bones. A search of the grounds turns up the burn site and the rest of the remains which have a gunshot wound to the sternum. Gasoline in the King's vintage car is a match for the accelerant.
- A post-mortem fracture to the hyoid came from the victim being dragged by a dog's choke chain. The angle of the break suggests the perpetrator was roughly the size of Mrs. King, while the trajectory of the gunshot wound indicates the perpetrator was significantly shorter.
- Lexie King's text messaging records reveal that on the night of Warren's death she was in the process of buying a project for school, which was against the strict honor code. Lexie admits that she shot the victim to keep her secret and her mom destroyed the evidence.

SPECIAL GUEST STARS: RYAN O'NEAL (MAX KEENAN), GINA TORRES (DR. TONI EZRALOW)
GUEST STARRING: MICHAEL GRANT TERRY (WENDELL BRAY), MOLLY HAGAN (ELSBETH KING), ROBIN THOMAS (RICHARD KING), JOHN LAFAYETTE (HEADMASTER DONNEGAN), AISHA HINDS (OFFICER NORMA RANDALL), HANNAH LEIGH DWORKIN (ALEXA KING), STERLING BEAUMAN (ROYCE KING), JOHN GRIFFIN (POACHER #1), RYAN MATTHEW (POACHER #2)

Brennan is uncomfortable when Cam hires her father, Max, as an instructor for a children's science program at the Jeffersonian without consulting with her first. Sweets points out this is probably because she is worried about her father abandoning her again. Even when Max assures her that he is not going anywhere, Brennan only relents when Booth asks her to let Max stay to help enrich Parker's education.

The backlog of episodes filmed prior to hiatus, combined with a rearranging of the airing schedule, resulted in 'The Bone that Blew' being the eleventh episode to air in the fourth season even though it was the second episode to be filmed. Coming into the fourth year of production on the show, many of the original crewmembers were still in place. Having worked on over fifty episodes together, the *Bones* crew was enjoying the benefits of their established team. Steve Beers explains, "What happens is that the longer you are working with the same people and breaking down the script and prepping an episode every eight days, the conversations become more streamlined.

Max: Science Squad, meet my daughter, the world famous anthropologist, Dr. Temperance Brennan. I taught her everything she knows.

Brennan: Actually, I went to college. I have multiple degrees.

Less time has to be taken talking about the kind of universal factors of the show: like the level of gore on the body or exactly what color palettes we like and don't like."

Jan DeWitt agrees, "In some respects, yes, there is a smoother rhythm. Staff and crew know when to expect scripts, meetings, meeting notes, budgets, etc. In episodic television, the department heads have more responsibility, so they know what they're doing and what is expected of them without being micro-managed. They know when and how to adjust to anything coming down the pipeline."

Conversely, continued success brings along its own set of problems. As the series grows, the audience's expectations grow as well, forcing the production to go big to satisfy the viewers. In season four alone, the show filmed an episode in an airplane mockup, went bungee jumping off a hot air balloon, created a circus, plus several small concerts. But as well as the large challenges, Steve Beers points out the simple day-to-day requirements of the series also become more challenging as time goes on. "The thing is, you need more time in some ways because once you've done something, you've done it," he notes. "Now you've got to find another way of doing it to keep it fresh. What you gain by streamlining is that it helps you deal with the fact that you're forever trying to find another way to do something."

Tetraethyl lead: An anti-knock additive in gasoline used in airplanes and vintage cars.

'The Sun Will Rise' by Brendan James, *The Day is Brave*

DOUBLE TROUBLE IN THE PANHANDLE

WRITTEN BY *LYLA OLIVER*   DIRECTED BY *DWIGHT LITTLE*

GUEST STARRING: RYAN CARTWRIGHT (VINCENT NIGEL-MURRAY), ED GALE (LAVELLE), LESTER "RASTA" SPEIGHT (MAGNUM), THE GREG WILSON (TUMBLES), BERNARD WHITE (DR. ALBERT MUIR), MAGEINA TOVAH (MADAME NINA), MAGGIE BAIRD (SANDRA HICKS), MICHAEL MONKS (DELL HICKS), STEPHEN LEE (TEXAS RANGER), MICHAEL PATRICK MCGILL (OKLAHOMA OFFICER), ANDY RICHTER (HENRY SIMON)

- Skeletal remains of conjoined twins are found in a shallow grave along the Texas/Oklahoma border. Decomposed cotton found with the victims suggests they were wrapped in a sheet. An online search for missing conjoined twins identifies the victims as circus performers Jenny and Julie Van Owen.

- Circus workers produce a note allegedly written by the twins explaining why they left the circus. Smudges and the slant of the writing indicate the letter was written by the left-handed twin, Jenny. However, the signatures of each girl were written with the incorrect hands, suggesting the letter was a fake.

- There are two complementary fractures on each of the victims' craniums as if their heads were cracked together. Approximate force to cause the fractures is 300 pounds per square inch, but there does not appear to be any other trauma from a weapon.

- Particulates of **magnesium carbonate** are found on the victims.

- Slight longitudinal fractures are found along the distal ends of all four fibulas and stress fractures on their **cuboids**. When Brennan steps out on the high wire, she realizes that the fractures came from the twins attempting to walk the wire. They would have fallen and smashed their heads together when they hit the net, killing them. The circus crew buried them out of respect and so the girls' parents would not sue.

Knowing that circus folk are a traditionally tight knit community, Booth and Brennan go undercover as performers in a knife-throwing act, hoping to be accepted into the group. The act is a hit, thanks largely to Brennan's trust in Booth and her pushing to make their performance more daring. Booth, however, is reluctant to put his partner in jeopardy in spite of him having the best knife skills in the Rangers.

Booth does get into the spirit of the circus, in spite of his aversion to clowns, but he cannot come close to matching Brennan's enthusiasm over their act. It's a change in her character that Emily Deschanel believes has been building for a while. "She's letting loose a lot more," she says. "Brennan gets really caught up in the performance and the attention. I loved playing the scene because it wasn't like anything Brennan had done before. She became more interested in doing their knife-throwing act than she was in solving the case. Bones would never have done that before!"

Along with her new attitude came a new style. Costume designer Molly MaGinnis joined the *Bones* crew on this episode and was instructed to freshen up the looks of all the characters—except Booth. Brennan, who had been dressed in "drab" and "murky" colors of late, was MaGinnis's primary concern. "They wanted to add more color and to bring more current style

Brennan: *Buck was more dashing than you. I mean, Buck drove a motorcycle.*

Booth: *Well, Wanda was funner than you.*

Brennan: *How?*

Booth: *Well, she let me knock off a rubber nose from her face with a knife. You would never let me do that. You're way too rational.*

into her look," she explains. "I knew they were going to be out in the desert in their regular clothes so the first thing I did was design a bright red safari-type jacket for her to wear so that we'd have a real burst of color out there. I think it helped. It made her a little more vibrant looking."

Also in need of added vibrancy, MaGinnis quickly learned that an extra splash of color could work wonders on the scenes set in the lab. As her predecessors had also discovered, the standard uniform of the Jeffersonian Medico-Legal lab was functional, but not necessarily fashionable, especially when you need to distinguish the characters from one another. "With television, there's lot of concentration on the area from the waist up," MaGinnis says. "So you just get that burst of whatever is framing the face. You really need to make a statement with that burst, especially if

they're going to be wearing lab coats a lot of the time. Because they always have that lab coat on so you really have to make the statement with the shirt. It's like a quick flash and you've got to get that across."

Nothing in this episode could possibly have been flashier than the circus scenes. Not only was the set lively onscreen, but it was off-screen as well. "The circus people were a kick," Steve Beers recalls. "That was an episode where I went out to my producer friends for help. Randy Zisk, over at *Monk,* had done a circus episode and he had liked [the people we ended up using] and gave me their number. It turned out that they were the people who had done *Carnivale*."

Once they had secured the circus performers, they needed to figure out the look for the circus. "We knew that we wanted the circus to be kind of threadbare,"

24 Hour Man: Comes to a new town ahead of the circus to make arrangements for the arrival.
Barber Act: Knife act
Clem: A fight
First of May: A newbie
Gilly: An outsider

Magnesium carbonate: Chalk used in flooring, fireproofing, cosmetics, gymnastics, and other powders.
Cuboid bone: A bone on the outer side of the foot.

'No Envy, No Fear' by Joshua Radin, *Simple Times*

Beers explains. "It was down on its luck. So we wanted it to be broken down, but we didn't want it to come off as very period in the way that *Carnivale* was. The real challenge was to find that balance." The production connected with various people in the L.A. area to get the right look. "The people that owned the tent, the rigging and so on, turned us on to this whole world of old circus performers and acrobats that live around L.A.'" notes Beers. "Some of them coached people for *Circus of the Stars*. There's this whole world out there that I had never been introduced to before. It was kind of funny because there's a carny aspect of doing a TV show. Your trucks pull into a neighborhood and invade. It was fun with those groups getting together."

"This was another fun set," set decorator Kimberly Wannop agrees. "L.A. Circus was so helpful in supplying us with the tents and the technical circus dressing. Michael Mayer designed the set into small vignettes. We had the main tent, the mess tent, the clown tent, the practice space, and then all of their campers and trailers that defined the outdoor space. We worked with the circus professionals in setting up the high wires and practice spaces. The clown tent was fun to decorate. We had makeup mirrors, tons of oversized clown props, wardrobe trunks, everything a clown would need. We also showed the transient stage that the circus people live in by showing how they just set up their little world wherever they go."

The look of the circus, like the costumes inside the lab, provided a splash of color in an otherwise nondescript setting. Taking place on and around the Texas/Oklahoma border, the production was tasked with creating a look that mirrored Middle America. Collectively, the team found that to be a much easier challenge in Southern California than trying to recreate the Washington D.C. area week after week. Steve Beers notes, "The great thing about that episode is that it was set in Texas. We could open the lens up, not only to where the circus was, but also to the motorcycle driving and the oil wells in the beginning. When the script is written to accommodate what you can just open up the lens and look at, it's always better than trying to manipulate the world in the way that we usually have to when we're saying that California is the East Coast. So that was great."

Location manager Stephen Weissberger was able to provide the producers with what they deemed to be the perfect spots for filming, without having to travel too far. "We filmed the discovery of the body and the house off Pico Canyon Road, near Santa Clarita—very close to where oil was first discovered in Southern California—about twenty-five miles north of Fox Studios. We filmed the circus scenes at the Hansen Dam Recreation Area in Lake View Terrace. We were actually very close to the dam itself for those scenes. Being in Los Angeles certainly helps: there are many different looks to choose from within the thirty-mile studio zone."

Unfortunately, not everything about the Hansen Dam location was as perfect as the producers had hoped. A wildfire encroached on the spot where the circus scenes were filmed, forcing the production to alter the filming schedule. "Luckily none of our crew or sets were harmed," Jan DeWitt says with relief. "But it was frightening nonetheless."

Henry Simon: And now direct from their triumphant tour of Europe and the Far East, Bingham's Circus of Wonders is proud to present the razor-sharp skills of the most thrilling, the most breathtaking, and the most dangerous knife-throwing act in the world. Ladies and Gentleman: Boris and Natasha and their Russian Knives of Death!

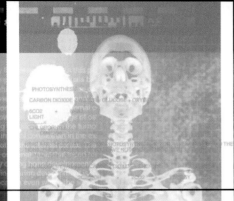

FIRE IN THE ICE

WRITTEN BY SCOTT WILLIAMS   DIRECTED BY CHAD LOWE

- The body of firefighter Pete Carlson is found under the ice of a frozen lake. Trauma to the left maxillary orbit suggests violence.
- Both of the victim's patellas are fractured, as if he was forced to his knees.
- Cause of death is likely a penetration to the **lacrimal sac** that went deep into the inferior orbital fissure.
- Deionized brine water, like that found in an ice rink, is found in the victim's esophagus, placing the rink as the murder scene.
- ALS reveals a large bloodstain on the ice as well as a blood trail indicating that the victim was dragged off. Blood drops run parallel to the smear, suggesting that the murderer was injured too.
- Ice samples are checked for a second set of DNA.
- Fish in the victim's home died of ammonia poisoning. Jewelry cleaned with amonia is found hidden under the fish tank gravel. The items were reported missing in a fire.
- It is determined that the victim and his volunteer firemen hockey teammates worked the jewelry store fire together. One of the friends, Ed Fralic, questioned the victim about the jewelry heist and ended up killing the man with a lace puller during their argument.

GUEST STARRING: PATRICIA BELCHER (CAROLINE JULIAN), MICHAEL GRANT TERRY (WENDELL BRAY), NATHAN WEST (ED FRALIC), STEPHEN MARTINES (ALEX PINA), NICK WARNOCK (DAVE SIMMS), JULIE DRETZIN (CONNIE WITHERS), BIANCA LAWSON (ALBIE), JHEMMA ZIEGLER (CHLOE BRATTON), THOMAS LUMBERG JR., (LOU HERRIN), JAMES DUMONT (LEN), JOSH BLAYLOCK (LEO), MARISA COUGHLAN (SPECIAL AGENT PAYTON PEROTTA), SPECIAL APPEARANCE BY: LUC ROBITAILLE (HIMSELF)

Much of 'Fire in the Ice' was filmed at Ice Station Valencia, a rink just north of Los Angeles. "It is one of the best ice arenas in Southern California," location manager Deborah Laub comments. "The facility has three rinks and we had total control of their NHL-sized rink for four days of filming. The owners and staff were terrific. They assisted us in every aspect of our episode including technical assistance, uniforms, and gear. They even allowed us to build the Chinese restaurant set in their banquet room."

It was especially fortuitous that the production had obtained such an easy location to work with because the action-packed episode was going to be a challenge to film on the ice. "We used every minute of every day that we were up there at Ice Station Valencia in order to get everything done," admits first assistant director Kent Genzlinger. "Any element: ice, water, kids, animals, whenever we throw that stuff in, it just multiplies your problems. Rehearsals take longer; everything like that. Chad Lowe directed that episode. He did an

Booth: Bones, what are you doing on the ice?

Brennan: I get nervous when you fall down and don't get up.

outstanding job and it really helped out that he is a hockey player. He actually plays hockey with Barry Josephson and David Boreanaz. We couldn't have done that episode if we hadn't had Chad and if David hadn't been a hockey player himself."

The episode also introduced another recurring character to the series in Agent Payton Perotta, someone that made the fans nervous right from her first scene. The fan reaction makes mischievous showrunner, Hart Hanson, chuckle. "You don't even have to set it up and everyone starts screaming, 'Oh no, here comes a love interest for Booth.' You couldn't ask for anything better than people jumping to that conclusion and going there because it means you don't have to write it."

Hanson won't comment on where he plans to take the character after season four, but he does confirm that she will be seen again. "She was wonderful," he says of both the character and the actress. "She's Brennan's opposite. She's warm. She's much more like a female version of Booth. She's much more compatible with him and that scares the crap out of everybody. The fact is we would have had her in more episodes this season, but she's very pregnant. So we'll look forward to seeing her in season five. I think she's a good addition. Not for every episode of course, but as another recurring guest actor."

Lacrimal sac: The dilated upper section of the nasolacrimal duct that receives tears from the lacrimal ducts.

'Double Down Under' by The Crystal Method

Weapon Identification

Forensic evidence found on a body can be useful in identifying the murder weapon, which is a central part of any investigation. Retrieval of the murder weapon not only answers the question of how the victim died, but it can also point directly to a killer.

Hand weapons are the cause behind a significant number of cases seen at the Jeffersonian Medico-Legal Laboratory. Any foreign object that attacks the human body is going to leave evidence of its presence. Whether from a bullet or a blade, wounds to the body and scrapes or gouges to the bone can be matched up with items in a suspect's possession to

identify a killer. Puncture wounds, kerf marks, contusions, and greenstick fractures are only some of the many informative scars that weapons leave behind.

Ballistics

Jeffersonian staff specialize in terminal ballistics: examining a bullet's effect on a body as opposed to the weapon itself. A bullet retrieved from a victim can be directly linked to the gun that fired it, due to the unique pattern of striae that forms on the bullet as it exits the barrel. Bullets retrieved from multiple victims can reveal a single murderer when linked to the same gun, as in 'The Con Man in the Meth Lab.' Even a bullet left in a body for decades will hold important clues to the weapon, as in the case of 'The Soccer Mom in the Mini-Van,' where records confirmed that a bullet retrieved years after a crime was committed matched the gun used in that crime.

Wounds left from a bullet's impact on a body also reveal telling information. The trajectory of a gunshot wound indicates the angle at which the bullet entered the body, which can reveal the location a shooter was firing from. In the case of 'The Bone that Blew,' the wound trajectory proved that the perpetrator was the height of a child. Gunshot residue found on the victim also reveals if a murderer was standing within five feet of the victim, as noted in 'The Girl in the Mask.' Conversely, the wound can impact on the

murder weapon as well. Shards of bone found in the barrel of the gun in 'The Baby in the Bough' proved that the weapon was fired at pointblank range and erased all doubt that it was the gun that killed the victim. DNA from flesh burned onto the gun matched the killer.

Tool Marks

Knives, clubs, and even medieval torture devices can leave distinct marks on the flesh and the bone. Matching a wound to the weapon that made its mark is an exact science aided by experience in the field. Dr. Brennan, for instance, can identify a hatchet wound by sight. A cast made from the cuts in the spine of a victim in 'The Girl in the Mask' allowed investigators to reverse engineer the knife

that had been used to sever the victim's head. Brennan immediately recognized the style of knife from past experience, which identified the man who severed the head, leading them to the actual killer. Conversely, the odd wound to the victim's skull in 'The Princess and the Pear' suggested a weapon that Brennan had never encountered before. That allowed her to dismiss all weapons that she did have experience with from the equation, narrowing down the field considerably.

The impact that a weapon has on a body also leaves valuable clues to the murderer. In the case of 'The Doctor in the Den,' investigators were able to determine that a snake hook was the murder weapon, based on measurements of the wounds. A computer recreation showed that the force necessary to inflict the wound came from a pole at least five-feet long with a diameter of ten centimeters being wielded by a person approximately five-feet seven-inches to five eleven-inches tall.

THE HERO IN THE HOLD

WRITTEN BY *JANET LIN & KARINE ROSENTHAL*
DIRECTED BY *IAN TOYNTON*

GUEST STARRING: BRENDAN FEHR (JARED BOOTH), NOEL FISHER (TEDDY PARKER), DEIRDRE LOVEJOY (AUSA HEATHER TAFFET), MARCO SANCHEZ (THOMAS VEGA), RICHARD LICATA (JUDGE WILLIAMS), MARISA COUGHLAN (SPECIAL AGENT PAYTON PEROTTA)

• When evidence is discovered to be missing in the Gravedigger case, Brennan, Hodgins, and former F.B.I. agent Thomas Vega are called in for questioning.

• The Gravedigger also suspects them of the theft and kidnaps Booth to offer in exchange for the evidence. Hodgins admits to Brennan that he has a shard of the bumper from the vehicle that struck him. The drop site for the evidence is rigged with explosives, which destroys the evidence.

• Vega is found dead in his car and Brennan convinces Jared Booth to use his connections to get her the body to autopsy.

• Vega's cause of death was a fatal fibrillation caused by a stun gun applied to the heart. Damage to the victim's right **ulna**, medial and lateral **epicondyles**, as well as his **coronoid fossa** are consistent with a defensive response to an assault from behind that likely broke his attacker's ribs. When AUSA Heather Taffet arrives at the lab, she cannot raise her arm, suggesting an injury consistent with the Gravedigger's offensive wounds.

• A storage locker owned by Taffet contains a pair of recently worn boots with traces of paint chips used in naval deck coating prior to 1961. This leads Brennan to a decommissioned naval ship prepping to be sunk to make a reef. She rescues Booth in the nick of time.

'The Hero in the Hold' was a story long in the making for *Bones*. The results of that wait are definitely seen onscreen in one of the largest episodes in the series' history. It was created as a sequel to the hugely popular second season episode 'Aliens in a Spaceship,' which saw Brennan and Hodgins fighting for their lives after being kidnapped and buried underground by a serial kidnapper with an unusual M.O., known as the Gravedigger.

Executive producer Stephen Nathan credits the genesis for the Gravedigger storyline as the writers' desire to come up against a particularly strong villain. "It started because we wanted to have a very, very smart antagonist," he explains. "We wanted to have someone who was as smart in a psychotic way as Brennan and Booth are in their ways. It was not the foolish kidnapper who is constantly in contact with people until you catch him. It was, I think, Hart's idea to make the kidnapper someone who delivers one message—one message only—in an untraceable manner, so that we could keep this story alive."

The Gravedigger's story picks up following the death of Assistant U.S. Attorney Kurland and the theft of a valuable piece of evidence in the case. The Gravedigger kidnaps Booth, offering to exchange him for the evidence that Hodgins stole in the hope that he would

have a better chance at making a break in the long floundering case.

As the team works to save Booth, he awakens trapped on a ship about to be sunk in the ocean. He struggles to escape the boat with help from the ghost of Teddy Parker, a man who died under his command. Teddy offers Booth forgiveness and asks him pass a message to his long lost love after he is rescued from the exploding boat. It is a rescue that arrives largely thanks to Brennan's persistence and his brother Jared's willingness to break the law to save his brother.

However, just because Booth is saved, it does not mean the story is over. Booth and his brother would see the ramifications of Jared's actions affect their relationship in the 'The Beaver in the Otter,' and Stephen Nathan promises that the larger case against the Gravedigger will continue past

the end of season four as well. "They had to skirt certain legalities in order to save Booth's life," he explains. "By doing that, the legal case against this woman is going to be in jeopardy because they have acted as rogues to a certain extent. They had to do it to save someone they loved, but at the same time they have compromised the case that the federal attorney has against the Gravedigger. We will be revisiting that next season. It is something that is still going to be up in the air."

The promise of returning to the storyline will give the actors more time to explore the emotions related to a case that had three members of the team in grave jeopardy. It is a storyline that TJ Thyne has been looking forward to playing out for Jack Hodgins. "I've been waiting for that Gravedigger to show up for two years!" he says. "The only sad part is that

Ulna: The thinner and longer of the two bones in the forearm.
Epicondyles: Protuberances at the elbow end of the humerus.
Coronoid fossa: A depression in the humerus that receives the coronoid process of the ulna when the forearm is flexed.

'When the Pain Dies Down' by Chris Stills, *Chris Stills*

we didn't get to see more of Jack's reaction and emotions during the Gravedigger return. Hart Hanson and I had discussed lots of different ideas about the Gravedigger coming back since we shot that episode in season two. So I was really looking very forward to that day."

One person who does get to unleash her anger toward the Gravedigger is the usually composed Dr. Brennan, who smashes the kidnapper on the head with a briefcase. "'The Hero in the Hold' was very different from a 'typical' *Bones* episode," notes Emily Deschanel. "I approached it like it was an action movie or a thriller. There's a clock ticking and we need to save someone we love. Brennan is very concerned about getting Booth back alive, but she knows that she can't break down emotionally because she needs to do her work to find him. You get a glimpse of how

she's feeling inside when she hits Taffet toward the end of the episode."

Brennan's attack is a small moment of action in a much larger episode that producer Jan DeWitt notes took several weeks to pull together. "We coordinated with many offices— U.S. Navy, Coast Guard, etc.—to bring everything together. One of the biggest problems was a rule that no helicopters could fly into the Port Hueneme Naval Base harbor. So with twenty-four hours left to go, I was finally able to collaborate with the base commander to get approval to fly the helicopter on and off the destroyer while in port. When the day finally came to shoot on the ship with the helicopter, it decided to rain on us. Our director and co-executive producer Ian Toynton remained flexible and made it all work once again so we could complete the episode we had all worked so hard on."

This, unfortunately, was not the only problem the production had to deal with. Steve Beers outlines the other issues they had to deal with: "There was a fire on the stage where we were shooting the water effects when we were prepping it that caused a great deal of turmoil," he explains. "The cooperation of the Navy with their helicopters was complicated by the wildfires that were going on. It was an absolute production nightmare from those points of view." But Beers notes that he still had a ball meeting the challenges the episode presented.

The co-executive producer particularly enjoyed figuring out how to fill the ship's hold with gallons and gallons of water, threatening Booth's life. He relates, "You have to figure, 'How can we do this without having to pump incredible levels of water into the set, which takes a long time and has to be heated so the actors don't get hypothermic.' My head went to an old trick of the train pulling out of the station. The trick is that you move the camera, not the train. When I thought about it, I realized we're reading the water going up a wall in the set. So we built the wall in sections. They were hidden by what looked like the superstructure of the ship, which was on hoists. We could film and then remove the section and drop the next section down on the hoist. We'd film there, getting closer to the door at the top, then remove that section, and drop it again on the hoist. We were able to make it look like the water was filling the room, but what was actually happening is the room was being lowered down into the water piece by piece. It was a solution that, time wise and money wise, really helped sell the water seeping into the boat."

Brennan: I find it ironic that you are, in effect, holding us hostage in order to catch the Gravedigger.

THE PRINCESS AND THE PEAR

WRITTEN BY *MATTHEW DONLAN & JEREMY MARTIN*
DIRECTED BY *STEVEN DEPAUL*

GUEST STARRING: *JOEL DAVID MOORE (COLIN FISHER), TARA BUCK (VALERIE DANIELS), ERIC NENNINGER (PETER KROON), OLIVER MUIRHEAD (BADGLEY MORMONT), BETSY RUE (SHINY KOPINSKY), CHARLES RAHI CHUN (BRUCE KIM), POETRI (CHIP DERF), CHARLIE STEWART (TREV THE MAGE), AUSTIN ROGERS (WARRIOR), MARISA COUGHLAN (SPECIAL AGENT PAYTON PEROTTA)*

- The body of a woman dressed as a fantasy character is found with severe damage to the skull. Trauma to the **mandibular**, **maxilla**, and the molars extends outward as if the weapon radiated symmetrically from the center of her mouth. A medieval torture device known as The Pear of Anguish fits the description of the murder weapon.
- A hand stamp from ImagiCon, a fantasy/science fiction convention, is found on the remains. Photos on the convention website include an image of a woman named Kendra Kim in the costume.
- The victim had been seen meeting with a wholesale importer of weaponry named Peter Kroon. He tells investigators that she was in possession of a valuable movie prop sword. Soil found in the victim's running shoes and under her fingers leads investigators to the buried sword.
- A collector named Valerie Daniels claims that the victim said someone "dressed as the Black Knight" gave her the sword on the first day of the convention.
- A man in a Black Knight costume attacks Brennan and Sweets while they have the sword. Brennan fights off the attacker, getting his blood on the blade.
- A piece of the attacker's chainmail is identified as a type manufactured by Peter Kroon. He admits to giving Kendra the sword because he loved her. He killed her when she dismissively tried to sell it.

Brennan reluctantly helps Booth with his back again, but injures him in the process and lays him up for the case. This minimized David Boreanaz's screen time in this episode as he was preparing to direct the next offering, 'The Bones that Foam.' Brennan awkwardly teams with Agent Perotta to crack the case.

"It's a very interesting episode," Hart Hanson notes, "because you always wonder how much could we remove either Brennan or Booth from an episode and still be an episode of *Bones*. I believe that despite everyone's good work, we really missed Booth in that episode. Next time he directs he's going to have to have two or three scenes less prep time."

'The Princess and the Pear' gave the audience more insight into both the uncomfortably morbid intern Colin and Dr. Lance Sweets via their participation in the convention world. As part of the arrangement to contribute profiling for cases, Sweets has been doing more fieldwork in season four, which John Francis Daley enjoys. "It's something I like to do because it gets me out of my office," the actor says. "But Sweets especially loves it because it's kind of the glamorized version of what he thought F.B.I. profiling would be when he first got into it. I think he has way more fun out in the field then he ever would talking to patients in his office."

Fantasy fans, like the ones seen in the episode, in reality aren't nearly as outside of the norm as some of the groups explored in the show, but it was a culture with its own look and language. Conveniently, costume designer Molly

Agent Payton Perotta: Dr. Brennan. Nice to see you. I was honored you requested me as a substitute for Agent Booth.

Brennan: The variables involved in breaking in a new person outweigh the benefit of possibly finding a better investigator.

Agent Payton Perotta: Let's not get gushy about it.

MaGinnis was already well versed in the styles of fantasy recreation. "I designed the film *Role Models*," she explains, "which also had a huge medieval fantasy segment. Luckily, I found a lot of sources that I had gone to for that movie and we were able to pull off a lot of great stuff. We tend not to have a lot of time to prep an episode, so it's all a question of finding the right resources—you have to know where to get chainmail."

While MaGinnis worked to outfit the convention attendees, other department heads were busy putting together the convention where they would gather. "We were looking for an event venue for the trade show sequences that was not simply a large empty convention floor warehouse," explains location manager Deborah Laub. "We found a former Wicke's Furniture Store that still had various display room dividers and hundreds of hanging track lights. These display room dividers gave the art department the 'bones' to work from to turn the former furniture store into ImagiCon."

Set decorator Kimberly Wannop took her job creating the look of that space very seriously, knowing that a large segment of the audience likely participated in that world and were acquainted with how it should look. "People really get into those conventions and are very dedicated to their fantasy games," she acknowledges. "I dressed about ten booths that all were different; some were costume, video games, weapons, and memorabilia. We made up an entire hero video game and had all the products made: such as the video game boxes, game display and posters."

Mandibular: The lower jawbone.
Maxilla: The upper jawbone.

'Grassy Mrs. Green' by Wasted Tape
'The Calendar Hung Itself' by Bright Eyes, *Fevers and Mirrors*

THE BONES THAT FOAM

WRITTEN BY ELIZABETH BENJAMIN   DIRECTED BY DAVID BOREANAZ

- A corpse found at the base of a gorge is identified off dental records as car salesman Alex Newcomb.
- The bones are becoming gelatinous and turning to foam at a six percent bone mass per hour rate of loss. It is later determined that the calcium in the bone is dissolving, which suggests that hydrofluoric acid had been applied to the body.
- The victim's brother and former coworker, Chet, informs investigators that the victim had recently changed jobs, moving to another car lot.
- A defect on the posterior aspect of the sternum suggests the victim was stabbed between the seventh and eighth vertebrae.
- Fecal matter from a monkey is found on the victim's shoes, confirming that he was at his former place of work, a jungle-themed car dealership, on the night of his murder. Evidence of blood is found in the dealership service area along with a barrel of corrosive tire cleaner that is sixty percent hydrofluoric acid, which would explain the condition of the foaming bones.
- Marks on the vertebrae indicates that the murder weapon was a pair of tailor shears, like those used by Chet Newcomb's seamstress wife, Vanessa. She agreed to sleep with Chet's boss in order for her husband to keep his job. The victim caught them and she killed him to stop him from telling Chet.

GUEST STARRING: RYAN CARTWRIGHT (VINCENT NIGEL-MURRAY), STONEY WESTMORELAND (JUNGLE JIM DELROY), ZACHARY KNIGHTON (CHET NEWCOMB), JANET VARNEY (MAUREEN PEROT), SUNKRISH BALA (BUDDY SHIRAZI), CHRISTINE LAKIN (VANESSA NEWCOMB), OMID ABTAHI (HAL SHIRAZI), RICH HUTCHMAN (KEVIN HOWARD), NICOLE MALGARINI (STRAWBERRY LUST), MICHAEL ADLER (PASTOR RICK)

While watching Booth interrogate a suspect, Brennan observes his innate ability to connect with people and asks Sweets to teach her how. Emily Deschanel remembers this scene very fondly. "There was a scene in which I ask Sweets to help me recognize human emotions from facial expressions," the actress relates. "Along with being very funny, that scene revealed so much about Bones. She really has no clue about human behavior, social interaction, etc."

It was a memorable scene for both Deschanel and John Francis Daley in an episode directed by their cast mate. David Boreanaz had directed for television before in his previous series, *Angel*, but this was the first time he had done so on *Bones*. "I've never seen David happier, or with more passion and enthusiasm, than when he directed that episode," notes Deschanel. "He has a natural talent for it. He was very respectful and gave me good notes as an actor. I knew he'd be a good director, but he exceeded my expectations."

Daley agrees wholeheartedly, and he also cites that particular scene between Sweets and Brennan as his own personal standout. "David could not have been better," he says. "He is definitely an actor's director. David helped in that scene by just making it the most relaxed kind of loose environment that allowed us to interact. We did cross coverage so we were filming on either side of us at the same time so that spark is still there. Everything that you see between us is going on in real time. It was a lot of fun."

Boreanaz impressed the cast and crew with his work throughout filming. "I think it took us all a minute to realize that his actor hat had been taken off," Tamara Taylor says. "He's a really good director.

Booth: Foaming? What would cause that? Too much beer? Or maybe he ate soap?

Brennan: You should stop using cartoons as a scientific reference point.

Intelligent actors tend to be good directors and he is such an intelligent actor and really is committed to exploring every nuance. He's open. He was a really wonderful, insightful, generous director."

Not everyone was as happy to learn that Boreanaz's first outing as a director for the show was such a success. Hart Hanson sees the downside of his actor's additional talent. "The only trouble is he made it look fun and easy, because he makes everything look fun and easy and now everyone's going to want to do it. Damn that David Boreanaz!" Hanson laughs.

Though in all seriousness, the series creator could not have been happier with the outcome. "I've said it before and I will keep saying it," Hanson continues, "I thought he would be a competent director; I thought he would do a fine job. I worried that as he's such a kinetic, bouncy guy he was going to have trouble concentrating and focusing as much as a

director has to—which is every second—instead of being like an actor where you can bounce off the walls until they yell 'action' then focus and then they're unfocused again. But he amazed me. I was completely and utterly shocked by his ability to focus and adapt to the exigencies of directing an episode.

"Everything changes all the time. The hours are brutal and you have to think of production things, not just creative things. An actor just gets to think about the creative side. I thought he was going to hate it when we said, 'You can't have a crane here' and 'No, that's too many people' and 'No, you don't get to do that.' He was absolutely flexible and pliable and he came up with incredibly creative ways to deal with the usual obstructions to making a good episode of TV. He's one of our best directors. I would recommend him for pilots. I thought he did a fabulous job. I was so relieved."

 'Stuck to You' by Nikka Costa, *Pebble to a Pearl*

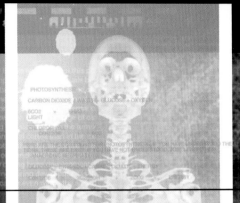

THE SALT IN THE WOUNDS

WRITTEN BY CARLA KETTNER & JOSH BERMAN
DIRECTED BY STEVEN DEPAUL

SPECIAL GUEST STAR: SPENCER BRESLIN (CLINTON GILMOUR)
GUEST STARRING: MONIQUE COLEMAN (BECCA HEDGEPETH), PEJ VAHDAT (ARASTOO VAZIRI), KAYLA EWELL (ALYSSA HOWARD), ANDREW BORBA (BOB CLARK), AMY PIETZ (ELLEN CLARK), RAMON DE OCAMPO (DR. SEAN FITTS), MATT BUSHELL (COACH ADAM HAWTHORNE), BRANDO EATON (RORY DAVIS), EARNESTINE PHILLIPS (TESS), HEIDI SULZMAN (DARLENE), NICHOLE HILTZ (ROXIE LYON)

- A body is found among the road salt in a city maintenance storage unit. The salt has desiccated the body, but the description matches missing high school volleyball player Ashley Clark.
- Blood chemistry shows an unusually high level of relaxin, a naturally occurring hormone secreted during pregnancy. Investigators quickly discover that numerous girls on Ashley's volleyball team are also pregnant.
- A hairline fracture is found on the **stapes** and there is a peri-mortem bruise to the surrounding tissue directly above the **vagus nerve**. When the vagus nerve is triggered with enough force, the victim will go into cardiac arrest and die. Considering the chances of hitting the nerve by accident are very slight, it suggests that the murderer knew what he was doing.
- Red fibers in the victim's hair are from a late model German sedan. Ashley's chiropractor drives such a car.
- Sweets and Angela go undercover to meet the chiropractor and they find a tool in his office that could be the murder weapon.
- Ashley seduced the chiropractor then threatened to charge him with statutory rape if he didn't pay her five thousand dollars that was a component of the pregnancy pact she'd entered into with her friends.

Booth and Brennan come across what appears to be a pact among teenaged girls to get pregnant and raise their children together. The case sounds very much like the rumored real-life pact between a group of girls in a Massachusetts high school. "We don't normally do ripped from the headlines," Stephen Nathan notes, "But [consulting producer] Josh Berman kind of spearheaded that episode with the pregnancy pact. I think it worked well for us. It was an interesting and bizarre event and it was fun to turn that into a mystery. We have done that a few times on the show, like we did the Scott Peterson thing and then really made that bizarre. We've done it a few times, but not all that much."

Angela is also contemplating the responsibilities of caring for another life. In her case, she's considering getting a dog that she will share with Roxie. Her girlfriend, however, sees this as a warning sign and a reminder that Angela is not somone who tends to stick around for the long haul. Roxie ends their relationship before their moment has passed, and Angela reacts by falling into bed with Hodgins. Worried about what her

Booth: ...This school ever heard of sex education?

Brennan: If so, there are gaps in the curriculum.

penchant for living in the moment means for her, Angela seeks advice from her friends. Sweets councils her that maybe it would be best to remove sex from the situation if that is what seems to be causing her confusion, suggesting that she should try celibacy for a while.

Music is often used to underscore the drama in *Bones* and this epiode is no exception. Music supervisor Kevin Edelman is charged with finding the right song to fit the mood for every episode, but he admits that it is a collaborative effort that begins with the script. "Sometimes songs are included in the script," he explains, "and other times the writer might just leave a slot for a great piece of music by writing something like, 'cool moody song plays as...' Other times, music just organically works into the cut. I typically work closely with editorial, so they can incorporate music as they cut the episode. This is the most natural way to integrate songs into each episode."

Edelman, logically, bases his music choices on what is going on with the characters in each episode, but he believes that the moody, edgy sound of singer-songwriters is what works best for the show. "I give the executive producers tremendous credit for recognizing great songs that play well in the show, even if they haven't heard it playing on Top 40 radio. I was very happy when we placed a José González song prominently in this episode. I've really enjoyed his music for a while, but hadn't had an opportunity to use anything until then."

Stapes: A small, stirrup-shaped bone in the middle ear.

Vagus nerve: The tenth of twelve paired cranial nerves that supply the organs of the chest and abdomen.

'Control Me' by The A-Team
'Friendly' by Christian Lundberg
'Heartbeats' by José González, *Veneer*
'Brand New Day' by Colin Armstrong

THE DOCTOR IN THE DEN

WRITTEN BY JANET LIN & KARINE ROSENTHAL
DIRECTED BY IAN TOYNTON

GUEST STARRING: EUGENE BYRD (DR. CLARK EDISON), DANA DAVIS (MICHELLE WELTON), REBECCA WISOCKY (DR. MAURA BAILEY), LINDA PURL (MRS. DIANA ANNENBURG), AUDREY WASILEWSKI (TRYSTA), CANDICE COKE (DR. NORA OLDHOUSE), DRU MOUSER (NANCY LAUDER) CHRISTOPHER NEIMAN (LANGSTON), PAMELA DUNLAP (MRS. JENKINS), JOEY ADAMS (DR. RICK ANNENBERG), CHAD LOWE (BRANDON CASEY)

- Human remains are found in the tiger habitat at a wildlife park. Bloodstaining around gnaw marks on the femur, but no fresh bleeding from the bone, indicates that the tiger fed on the victim post-mortem. Dental records are matched to Dr. Andrew Welton, a surgeon at a hospital that recently held a fundraiser at the park.
- There is evidence that a weapon sliced along the victim's right pelvis and thigh, transecting the **femoral artery**, leading the victim to bleed to death. A shoelace, tied in a knot, is mixed in with the flesh.
- White flecks embedded in the pelvic bone are polymerized hydrocarbon, from the serrated edge of a plastic knife. It is believed that the knife was used to enlarge the initial wound to treat the victim. The shoelace had probably been used to tie off the femoral artery to stop the bleeding, indicating someone with a medical background was involved.
- A snake hook at the reptile shed is consistent with the victim's wound, suggesting it is the murder weapon. The snake scales, however, come from a snake not native to the park, suggesting that it came from a shoe or other accessory.
- Photos from the benefit show nurse Nancy Lauder is carrying a snakeskin purse with a gauge in it. She admits to the murder as a reaction to the victim's philandering.

Another case hits close to home when the victim is a man from Cam's past named Andrew Welton. The pair lived together for two years, and during that time Cam was the *de facto* mother to the victim's young daughter, Michelle. The now teenage girl acts like she doesn't remember Cam, but it's a ruse to cover her anger over her feelings of abandonment when Cam and Welton broke up. Cam ultimately realizes that Michelle still cares for her and offers to adopt the girl.

Bones is a series that primarily follows the relationship between the two main

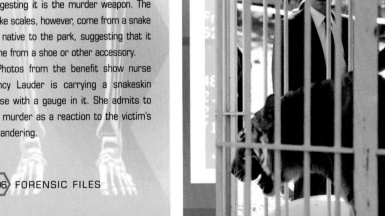

characters of Brennan and Booth. But there is also a talented ensemble integral to every episode that the audience follows as well, watching their lives play out in subplots alongside each main storyline. Hart Hanson realizes how important this ensemble cast is to the show and strives to give each member their day in the sun by periodically focusing episodes on them as well. "You want everybody to have an episode that's kind of *their* episode; aside from Booth and Brennan for whom every episode is their episode," Hanson explains. "It was time for Tamara to have her chance at that. We'd known about this story for quite some time: that we would have someone from Cam's past with a daughter that Cam would end up being responsible for. Tamara is so wonderful in this episode that you just know you're going to want to see this story unfold."

The wonderful thing about these "spotlight" episodes is that it gives the actors a chance to work outside of the lab, exploring stories that have less to do with technical jargon and corpses. "In a way, poor Tamara–all of the Squints to be fair.

Booth: Come on, Bones, you gotta take time to smell the primates.

Brennan: Why? They're malodorous and they throw their excrement.

The fact that they make those lab scenes so interesting is a testament to how very, very versatile and charismatic they all are," Hanson continues. "It's not the seat of great drama: looking at dead bodies and saying what has killed them. They have to bring so much craft and art and appeal to it. And they all do that."

Tamara Taylor was thrilled to play the new dynamic to her character, but it did require a shift in her thinking. "We're pretty thorough actors and we're all invested in the characters," she says. "We've been given certain information about them going in, and beyond that you elaborate within your own imagination. I created a whole backstory for Cam that sort of gets annihilated every time I get a new piece of information or a new story-line. 'Oh. Okay. I have a kid. Good to know. Didn't know that about myself.' It's fun and keeps you pretty nimble as an actor because I didn't know that storyline was coming until it came, so it wasn't anything I ever could have played before that."

As for this episode's subplot, Clark Edison makes another return trip to the Jeffersonian with Brennan's assurance that he will not have to mix the professional with the personal. Angela is following through with the plan for celibacy, which is making her particularly inappropriate around Clark. He brings in his girlfriend to set Angela straight, but it all goes wrong for him when the conversation turns to ways Angela can help herself.

Femoral artery: A large artery in the muscles of the thigh.

'In the Jungle' by Rootz Underground, *Movement*

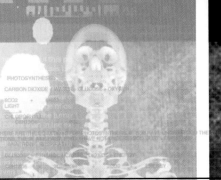

THE SCIENCE IN THE PHYSICIST

WRITTEN BY KARINA CSOLTY   *DIRECTED BY* BRAD TURNER

GUEST STARRING: RYAN CARTWRIGHT (VINCENT NIGEL-MURRAY), JOHN PYPER-FERGUSON (DR. LANDIS COLLAR), AIMEE GARCIA (JENNIFER KEATING), ANIL RAMAN (DR. CHRISTOPHER BEAUDETTE), AUGUST EMERSON (MILTON ALVARADO), JASON ROGEL (BRODERICK MULLINS), BILLY F. GIBBONS (ANGELA'S DAD), ARIELLE VANDENBERG (MODEL), SHAWN CARTER PETERSON (PHOTOGRAPHER)

- A garbage bag filled with human remains in numerous pieces no bigger than a softball is found in a vacant lot. Absence of hemorrhagic tissues indicates that the victim was dead before being disassembled. The victim's cells burst from the inside out, as would be experienced during freezing.
- A piece of meteorite matching a sample on display at the Collar Institute is found in the remains. Dr. Landis Collar immediately identifies the meteorite as being from the engagement ring worn by his fiancée, Dr. Diane Sidman. Collar suggests investigators speak with the victim's students, Milton Alvarado and Jennifer Keating.
- Cylindrical notches in the clavicle contain minute traces of graphite, clay, and copolymer, suggesting a mechanical pencil to the throat was the cause of death.
- There are over 300 fractures on the body. Each fracture happened at the weakest point of each bone, suggesting that the bones were shattered by vibration, as would occur in a resonance chamber.
- The presence of pond scum—which is part of Milton Alvarado's experiments—proves the student had been in the Collar Institute's resonance chamber. Minute traces of the victim's blood are found in one of Alvarado's mechanical pencils. He murdered the victim because she refused to publish his work in the noted Collar Journal unless he shared credit with her.

The Collar Institute, a center for advanced scientific research, is the centerpiece to 'The Science in the Physicist.' Introduced as a school of science that turned down Brennan for a fellowship years earlier, because her field looked to the past rather than the future, it is set up as a brain trust where Booth is meant to feel out of place. In addition to their higher than average intelligence, the scientists at the institute have a very matter-of-fact approach to sexual relations—separating it from emotions.

The fact that Brennan seems right at home in the world that Booth describes as "creepy" provides another situation that challenges their opposing views of the world and cuts to the heart of their relationship. In the end, Booth helps her understand that his description of the place had nothing to do with her, and more to do with how he felt out of his

element. Unfortunately, Brennan's attempt to comment on his intelligence isn't nearly as convincing.

Being that the Collar Institute is central to the episode, the production needed to find the right location for the property. The location manager was able to find a children's museum in Lakeview Terrace that was the perfect setting for the institute. Even better, they had a blank slate to work with since the museum hadn't moved in yet. "It's a great building that was still under construction," first assistant director Kent Genzlinger explains. "We were able to go in and have Michael Mayer dress up the place. It has a fascinating look to it and lots of great angles that ended up giving the show a really strong look."

The episode is also notable for Hodgins conducting not one, but *two* experiments. This is surprising considering how reluctant he'd been to do any at all at

Cam: It's obvious. He was frostbitten while climbing Everest, then struck by a meteor, then dumped into a vacant lot in two garbage bags, and eaten by crows.

Booth: Right, obvious. That's so obvious.

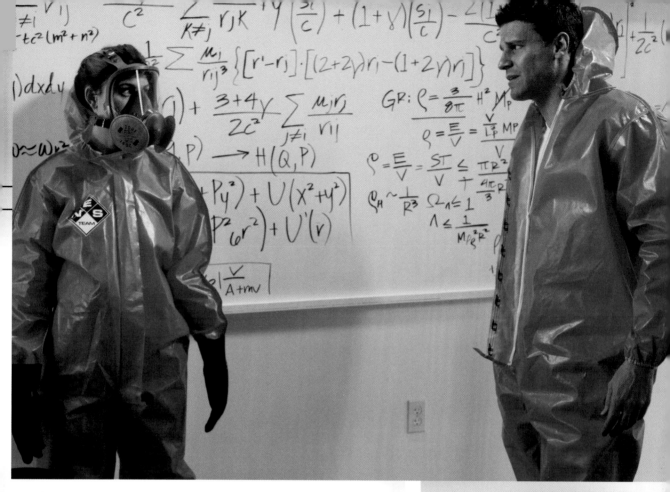

the start of the season. Granted, Cam would probably have preferred him to do neither, since one required him to fire a cannon indoors, and the other ended up with Angela being beaned by a frozen turkey. In a combination of a physical and visual effects, the turkey was added in later. Co-executive producer Steve Beers breaks down the effect: "When the turkey bounced up and clipped Angela and spun a light it went passed, that was a physical effect. Then the turkey was added in visual effects."

As well as a wayward frozen turkey, Angela also had to deal with her father coming to town to have a word with Hodgins about their breakup. Even though Angela speaks with her dad, it doesn't stop him from exacting some revenge. Hodgins wakes up in the middle of the desert in Mexico with a tattoo that reads "Angie Forever."

The return of Angela's dad caused tension onscreen, but Michaela Conlin says that the return of ZZ Top guitarist Billy F. Gibbons to the show could not have been more welcome behind the scenes. "He's the loveliest guy ever," she says. "He had been on tour since the wedding episode, which was the end of season two. He's like the hardest working guy in show business." Looking back on the episode Conlin recalls her first thoughts when she found out how her dad intended to exact his revenge on Hodgins. She explains: "I was like, 'Oh god, does that mean I'm going to have to get a matching tattoo?'"

'El Diablo' by ZZ Top, *Tejas*

THE CINDERELLA IN THE CARDBOARD

WRITTEN BY *CARLA KETTNER & JOSH BERMAN*
DIRECTED BY *STEVEN DEPAUL*

GUEST STARRING: MICHAEL GRANT TERRY (WENDELL BRAY), CARLA GALLO (DAISY WICK), KEVIN CHRISTY (KURTIS ROSSI), LINDA HART (MRS. LUCINDA BERTOLINO), ERIC MATHENY (BOB CAVERLY), PAT LENTZ (ANYA PERTEL), PJ BYRNE (JOE FILLION), MAYIM BIALIK (GENIE GORMON), BRANDON SCOTT (BARTENDER), MATTHEW YANG KING (DR. MARCUS SCHEER), JERRY ZATARAIN JR. (JUAN), RENÉ L. MORENO (BARNEY)

- A woman's crushed remains are found pressed into a cardboard bale at a recycling center. The second joints on the victim's middle toes have been shaved in a rare procedure that leads to a podiatric surgeon who identifies the victim as bride-to-be Meriel Mitsakos.

- The victim's clothes have a layer of glycerin on them and the cardboard boxes the body was pressed between came from a nightclub that uses bubbles made of glycerin. Gravel in the back alley of the club matches that found on the victim. The victim's damaged cell phone is found in the alley along with blood.

- The cell phone is linked to the Date or Hate dating service, which leads to founder, Kurtis Rossi. Records indicate the victim accepted a date request from a man named Owen Smith on the night she died.

- There is peri-mortem bruising to the victim's head with a distinct SUV tire tread. Patellar fractures fifty-four centimeters high are consistent with being struck by a bumper. The wounds posit a scenario in which the victim was struck once, knocked down, and then run over.

- A photo of Owen Smith proves to be a composite of several photos of the men that the victim had previously agreed to date. This leads to company founder Kurtis Rossi, who admits he created the persona in hopes of getting a date—and killed the victim when she rejected him.

What is initially believed to be the image of the Virgin Mary in cardboard turns out to be the grisly body of a bride-to-be in a case that, once again, gives Brennan and Booth the opportunity to debate the value of marriage. This time, Brennan seems to soften to the idea when she admits that she is jealous of her friends' feelings on the matter as she wants to believe in love, too. Booth assures her that one day she will.

Today, however, is not the day, as proven when both Brennan and Booth

see Sweets' girlfriend, Daisy Wick, trying on wedding gowns and hugging a man who is not their psychologist. Jumping to the wrong conclusion, Brennan wants to tell Sweets, but Booth and others try to convince her to stay out of it. However, valuing honesty, she does inform Sweets of the presumed betrayal. The news sends him into a depression over the perceived cheating and his own inability to see it, until he finds out it was all a big misunderstanding.

The relationship between Sweets and Daisy may have been a surprise to the other characters on the show, but the actor playing the young psychologist understands his character's motivation. "Daisy and Sweets sympathize with each other for being annoying to the other characters. But they also share intelligence and they're both very innocent and sweet, especially to each other," John Francis Daley says. The depth of Sweets' feelings are made clear in this episode from the way Brennan's news jolts him to the core. "When my character learns that Daisy is possibly

Daisy: I can only imagine what it would be like to have your brain.

Brennan: That's true.

cheating on him or is actually engaged to another man, I think it totally takes him by surprise," Daley continues. "He questions himself as a psychologist for not being able to see what was going on all along. Obviously, he finds out that nothing was going on and it kind of re-validates him. It's nice to be in one of the more stable relationships on television."

Hodgins is forced to make his own very personal admission when a clue in the case reveals that he's signed on for a matchmaking service. Angela signs up as well, but when the service matches the two of them up, both former lovers decline the chance to get back together. It's a difficult decision for both the characters, but TJ Thyne notes that things are particularly tough for Hodgins. "For four years Jack has been pining for her," he says. "At some point, after three proposals and unending devotion he's starting to think, 'Hold up... is this unrequited love, the most painful of all love?' Guys put up a strong front. We have to; society demands it of us. But when you meet the one, truly *the one*, as Jack has met in Angela, then our insides simply melt when they walk by. A single look from her and you stop breathing for a few minutes. A single soft touch to the shoulder could knock us out cold for weeks. That's Jack. That's Angela, to Jack."

'Life Boat' by Miranda Lee Richards, *Light of X*

Psychological Profiling

Dr. Lance Sweets holds multiple degrees in abnormal psychology, clinical psychology, and behavioral analysis. He is the youngest F.B.I. profiler on staff and works almost exclusively on cases at the request of Special Agent Seeley Booth. Considered an expert in his field, Dr. Sweets has helped in a number of cases and has provided expert testimony in court based on his findings. Booth's partner, noted forensic anthropologist Dr. Temperance Brennan gives little credence to the soft science of psychology, but even she has been coming around to the young psychologist after seeing the benefits of his work in the field.

Most notable among Dr. Sweets' professional work was the criminal profile he developed on the Gormogon killer, agreeing with a layman's supposition that the killer believed that he was doing important work—ridding the world of the secret societies that control people's lives. Though Sweets failed at identifying the killer's apprentice, he was correct in knowing that the Gormogon himself was no one important: "an invisible man, angry at history for not seeing him."

Using visual tells combined with suspect statements during interviews, Dr. Sweets works up a psychological profile of an individual to guide investigators in their search for the truth. Sweets also takes external factors relevant to the case and the knowledge of typical human behavior into account in working up his evaluation. It is not an absolute science, but Sweets' observations have proven correct more often than not, even though his voice has not always been heard. In the case seen in season three's 'The Wanna-be in the Weeds' Sweets' warnings of the danger of a potential stalker were ignored with near fatal consequences.

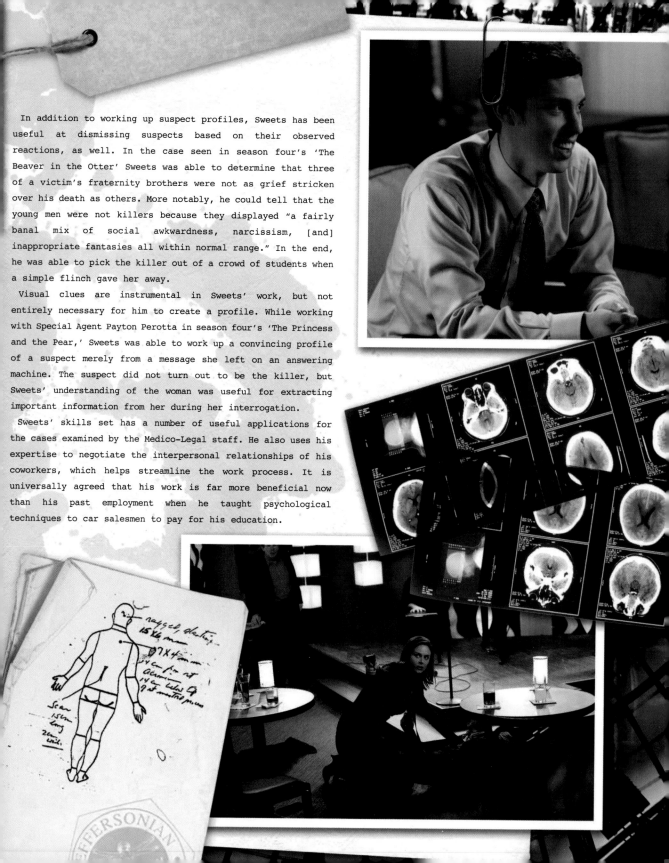

In addition to working up suspect profiles, Sweets has been useful at dismissing suspects based on their observed reactions, as well. In the case seen in season four's 'The Beaver in the Otter' Sweets was able to determine that three of a victim's fraternity brothers were not as grief stricken over his death as others. More notably, he could tell that the young men were not killers because they displayed "a fairly banal mix of social awkwardness, narcissism, [and] inappropriate fantasies all within normal range." In the end, he was able to pick the killer out of a crowd of students when a simple flinch gave her away.

Visual clues are instrumental in Sweets' work, but not entirely necessary for him to create a profile. While working with Special Agent Payton Perotta in season four's 'The Princess and the Pear,' Sweets was able to work up a convincing profile of a suspect merely from a message she left on an answering machine. The suspect did not turn out to be the killer, but Sweets' understanding of the woman was useful for extracting important information from her during her interrogation.

Sweets' skills set has a number of useful applications for the cases examined by the Medico-Legal staff. He also uses his expertise to negotiate the interpersonal relationships of his coworkers, which helps streamline the work process. It is universally agreed that his work is far more beneficial now than his past employment when he taught psychological techniques to car salesmen to pay for his education.

MAYHEM ON A CROSS

WRITTEN BY *DEAN LOPATA*   DIRECTED BY *JEFF WOOLNOUGH*

SPECIAL GUEST STAR: *STEPHEN FRY (DR. GORDON WYATT)*
GUEST STARRING: *EUGENE BYRD (DR. CLARK EDISON), A.J. TRAUTH (PINWORM), MICHAEL WILLIAM FREEMAN (GRINDER), TANIA RAYMONDE (LEXI), GREG ROMAN (MURDERBREATH), FRIDA FARRELL (DR. SOLBERG), THOR KNAI (DELTA UNIT COMMANDER)*

- Human remains found tied to a cross in Norway are shipped back to the U.S. when it is determined that the victim is an American citizen who died on U.S. soil. The remains were in the possession of a Norwegian black metal band that claims they stole them from an American band.

- Staining on the skull is common theatrical makeup. Extrapolating from the makeup stains, Angela creates a rendering of the victim's appearance when he died, runs it through an image search of metal web pages and comes up with a bassist named Mayhem in a band called Spew. Other band members, Monty Bigelow, Matt Stickney, and Darrel Moss, identify the victim as Justin Dancy.

- A wound to the gluteus is consistent with a prior gunshot injury that healed around the bullet, which was removed from the victim upon his death. It is suspected that the killer kept the bullet as a trophy.

- Wounds to the neck and a puncture to the posterior side of the C-5 vertebra suggest that the victim was garroted with barbed wire.

- The victim's ex-girlfriend, Lexi, reveals that she left the death metal world to go power punk, which some would consider selling out. She thinks someone killed Justin when they found out he wanted to join her band and leave the scene.

- Spew band member Pinworm wears a bullet around his neck. It is consistent with the mark left in the victim's **ilium**.

Dr. Gordon Wyatt returns to meet with Dr. Sweets to discuss the book he's writing on Booth and Brennan. Wyatt admits to Sweets that he doesn't share Sweets' deeper calling to the profession, which is why he is retiring.

Sweets reveals that he was into death metal as a teen and he even gets into character to fit in during a concert. Brennan sees scars on his back when she uses his shirt to staunch the blood on an accident victim. Wyatt enlightens Booth and Brennan on the darkness in Sweets' past so they will try harder to befriend the young shrink.

"Believe it or not, I had no idea that he had such a troubled backstory until I read the script for 'Mayhem on a Cross.'" John Francis Daley admits. "But I think it's okay in terms of how I had been portraying the character because I don't think Sweets would ever let that show. Even if I did know about what had occurred, I think that he would be so buttoned up and reserved about that whole side of his life that you would never guess that he had to endure anything hard. Which makes it all the more interesting that now, all of a sudden, we're seeing this side of him that we'd never seen before. I'm interested to see if they take it any further in terms of what he's had to deal with and if he's willing to tell them any more than he has."

"It's quite a moving story with Sweets' past," says Stephen Nathan. "We laid in that he was adopted during the circus show ['Double Trouble in the Panhandle'] and then in 'Mayhem on a Cross' we moved that a little further along in seeing he had a complicated childhood: when he was adopted he was essentially rescued." Nathan notes the benefits of delving deeper into the histories of the series' supporting characters: "They're characters that we laugh at, or laugh with, and then all of a sudden we find that they have a lot more underneath then we initially thought. I think it just draws the audience closer to those characters and makes them more invested in the show."

The episode, which gave greater insight into Sweets, Booth, and Brennan, also explored another interesting subculture that the audience at large probably knew little about. Once again, this provided interesting challenges for the production staff. Music supervisor Kevin Edelman, who generally prefers the sounds of the singer-songwriter for the show, had to delve into a very different kind of music not usually considered when setting the mood for the scenes. "This was a fun music episode," Edelman says. "We used music from real bands to represent the fictitious bands in the episode. I did a wide search and found some really great authentic black metal that we licensed for the episode. Coincidentally, two of the band members that were cast to be in the band, Zorch, are actually in the real band whose music we licensed. That was a fine case of the stars aligning."

"I think it's a tremendous episode," Steve Beers raves. "It had a lot of serendipity about it. The music was great.

Ilium: The large, broad bone that forms the upper portion of the pelvis.

'Better' by Blue Shoes, *The Best of Blue Shoes*
'Get to the Choppah' by Jameson, *Down for the Count*
'God of Anger' by Droid, *Droid*
'Turn to Dust' by Tondra Soul

The sideline musicians that came in were incredible. A couple of bands were featured that were a mixture of real heavy metal musicians and actors. The musicians were so good with the actors, teaching them how to cheat in no time at all. We had an afternoon of rehearsing and it was just phenomenal how they melded with each other. These guys would go, 'No, all you have to do is this, this, and this, and you'll sell it.' It was the absolute accident of getting so many people who were so right for what we were trying to do. They not only did what we were asking of them, but were an incredible help, pushing things along by coaching the non-musicians, and by the kind of energy they brought to it."

The stars also aligned for the prop department: prop master Ian Scheibel explains that he discovered that he didn't have to go far for research. "My assistant, Dave Rottenberg, toured with Nine Inch Nails and *is* that subculture," Scheibel explains. "So he was pretty much in charge of procuring all the black metal instruments. Throw in some barbed-wire necklaces and a few inverted crosses and *voila*."

Costume designer Molly MaGinnis didn't have the good fortune of an expert in the genre on staff, but her approach to creating the bands' looks was really no different from her usual approach. "We did a lot of research on that because each type of metal band has

their specific look so we were trying to accomplish that in order to differentiate the bands," she says. "Every project you do involves some kind of research. Whether it's just doing people who park cars at a country club to death metal bands, you always have to do your research, bring some reality to it and then make the character."

For one area of the production, research duties were pretty light for this episode as location manager Deborah Laub already had a place in her files that would be perfect. The Southern California Edison Eagle Rock Substation provided moody settings for various scenes in season three's 'Mummy in the Maze' and it would prove equally useful for this episode. "We shot it for the opening sequence Norwegian metal band concert, the slaughterhouse concert, the underground club concert and the Spew concert video," she recounts. "It's a terrific building that works for all sorts of dark, bleak, dungeon-like locations. Believe it or not, we still have a couple of rooms we haven't shot yet."

"It was one of those situations where this old, abandoned power station gave us three sets that felt very different from each other," Steve Beers adds, continuing his account of how everything seemed to come together perfectly for this episode. "The extras that Central Casting got together for us were brilliant. The people that showed up with a decidedly metal looks—and I mean hardcore—were wonderful to work with. The director had a great spirit. The A.D.s were great with these people. It was an incredible amount of work, but it all flowed and everyone seemed to really enjoy it. It was a hard thing to pull off and yet, at the end of that day, I remember just feeling so satisfied by what we had accomplished."

Booth: You're gonna be a chef?

Dr. Gordon Wyatt: That is correct, yes. I'm going to put good things into people instead of taking out things that are bad. I know it's a little Freudian, but Sigmund's been largely discredited, so to Hell with him.

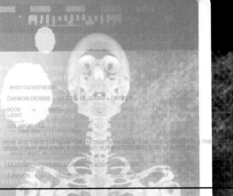

THE DOUBLE DEATH OF THE DEARLY DEPARTED

WRITTEN BY CRAIG SILVERSTEIN   DIRECTED BY MILAN CHEYLOV

GUEST STARRING: KELVIN YU (FRANKLIN TUNG), KATHRYN MEISLE (HELEN REILLY), ELLEN GEER (ANNIE REILLY), MATT MALLOY (BARNEY REILLY), MANDY SIEGFRIED (AMY VALESKA), RYAN MICHELLE BATHE (ERIN MILLER), DALE GODBOLDO (DR. JONAH AMAYO), KAZUMI AIHARA (TRACI NISHIMURA)

- At the wake of a coworker who supposedly died of heart failure, Brennan sees evidence inconsistent with the reported cause of death. The sternum of the deceased, Hank Reilly, is cracked in a manner inconsistent with CPR.
- There is a large contusion on the skin above the victim's ribs. As there is no bruise on the coroner's report, it is believed that the victim was still alive at the time he was initially declared dead.
- Thirteen trocar buttons mask evidence of puncture sites caused by a weapon three-eights of an inch in diameter, most likely a standard medical trocar used in arterial embalming. The victim was stabbed seven times while he was still alive.
- The undertaker, Franklin Tung, admits that the man awakened while he was being embalmed. Tung panicked and stabbed him to death.
- A trace amount of tetrodotoxin is found in the **vitreous humor** of the eye. The poison can kill a victim up eight hours after it is injected. Until then, the body mimics death.
- The victim's half-brother, Barney, reveals that Hank was due to receive the bulk of an inheritance. Now it will be evenly split between Barney and Hank's wife, Helen.
- Traces of the poison are found in tea in the victim's home. When the victim's stepmother reacts to Brennan serving the tea at the funeral she reveals herself as the murderer.

The team attends a wake at the home of a coworker. When Brennan suspects murder, they are unable to get an injunction to examine the body, so they are forced to steal it to get it back to the lab.

"We shot at a house out in Alta Dena," Steve Beers explains. "That home was one of those situations where you walk in and go, 'This place is absolutely perfect!' It's perfect for who the character is, for what we have to stage there, and for the feeling of being on the East Coast. For as much work as we had out there, the space would keep fresh." The production did use the location to the fullest, shooting interiors and exteriors in and around the house.

"I love that episode," Stephen Nathan adds. "We had a new director [Milan Cheylov] who was just terrific. It's a really funny episode that was written by Craig Silverstein who is just so out there in the greatest way possible. It was such a good idea. So funny. The actors all had such a great time, running around with a dead body. We just tried to go right up to the edge and see how far we could get."

Hart Hanson echoes his producing partner's delight in the episode. "It's one of those ones where you go, 'Are we really going to do Weekend at Bernie's?'" he says. "And 'How are we going to walk the tight wire of tone?' I was really afraid that it would go too broad and we'd be goofy.

Brennan: There are no such things as zombies. It's just an island superstition.

Dr. Jonah Amayo: And now you've managed to insult an entire culture and their belief system.

Booth: She does that to everyone.

We are a slightly goofy show, I'm the first to admit it, but you don't want to be *really* goofy. You want to keep at least one foot on the ground. And they did a great job. My god, those people are good. Our cast is so good. Milan Cheylov did a great job directing them. It's one of the funniest episodes of *Bones* ever."

As the saying goes, "dying is easy, comedy is hard," and this episode would prove that to be true. Hanson states, "I say to everyone: 'Please god let the script be the most broad thing. Work inside the script. Don't go outside. Don't push the boundaries of the script.' My deal with the actors is we'll be really pretty crazy, but keep it inside the fence of the script. They did a great job of that and it's very funny. It's underplayed a bit so you don't feel like it's a Keystone Kops, because that's the danger if everybody just gets huge. But it didn't happen. I love my cast, I love them so much. That's one of the things where this really frees us up. We can do anything on this show and those two and the Squints will get it."

Vitreous humor: The transparent, jellylike tissue filling the eyeball behind the lens.

'Amazing Grace' performed by Emily Deschanel and cast
'Swing Low, Sweet Chariot' performed by David Boreanaz and cast

THE GIRL IN THE MASK

WRITTEN BY MICHAEL PETERSON   **DIRECTED BY** IAN TOYNTON

GUEST STARRING: BRIAN TEE (KEN NAKAMURA), ALLY MAKI (DR. HARU TANAKA), BUMPER ROBINSON (MICAH STRUTT), LARRY CLARKE (PAUL VOGLER), YUJI OKUMOTO (BRUCE TAKEDO), ROBERT WU (JAMES SOK), KATHERINE KAMHI (OFFICER LISA KOPEK)

- A car registered to Sachi Nakamura is found abandoned near the Tillbrook Salt Marshes. A Japanese anime mask in the marsh contains the decapitated head of Nakamura. The rest of her body is later found in another section of marsh. The victim's roommate, Nozomi Sato, is also missing.

- There is a contact wound inferior to the mandible, exiting slightly anterior to the **Bregma point**. A splinter of arrow bamboo is later found in the brain.

- James Sok, a pimp, admits that Sato works for him, but claims not to know Nakamura. Sato was last seen with a client named Paul Vogler.

- Aspiration of the lungs indicates the victim was drowned. A water sample from the lungs contains dibromides, an active ingredient in algaecides used in water features. It is conjectured that Nakamura was drowned, her head was severed, then mounted on a bamboo spike in Sato's mask as a warning.

- A cast made of the cut to the spine indicates that a marine knife was used to sever the head.

- A knife found on Sok's boat with blood in the casing proves that he cut off her head. Sok cuts a deal to reveal the murderer as Sato's client, Paul Vogler. He killed Nakamura when she threatened to call the cops if he ever hurt Sato again.

While Brennan works to narrow down her pool of interns to finally choose a replacement for Zack, Booth gets a call from an old friend in Tokyo. Ken Nakamura asks Booth to look in on his sister who is living in D.C. and has not called him for days. When the girl turns up dead, Nakamura comes to the U.S., bringing an attractive, androgynous associate, Dr. Haru Tanaka, to assist with the examination of the body. The Squints proceed to spend much of the case trying to figure out the doctor's gender. Angela eventually determines that he is male through a goodbye hug.

'The Girl in the Mask' is another episode that delved into an intriguing subculture and allowed the production to create interesting visuals onscreen. The investigation takes Booth and Brennan into a Japanese teen world of amaloli and kei teens who dress like anime characters come to life. "That was really interesting," first A.D. Kent Genzlinger says, "because you sometimes see images of that Japanese teen culture stuff, but we really got immersed in it. It was an eye opener. There's some pretty funky stuff that these kids dress up as and in the way they present themselves. Central Casting did a great job finding local teenagers who have either transferred from Japan or the culture has transferred to them and they've picked it up here. The kids we saw in that episode dressed as amaloli girls and the kei teenagers were all local L.A. background. They came with their own stuff and also referenced others in L.A. that were into that sort of scene."

As well as exploring the interesting visuals of the underground Japanese teen world, the production also depicted Japan itself onscreen, though, in fact, they never left the Fox lot for those scenes. Genzlinger explains, "We got to

Sweets: You people can identify human remains based on a tiny little finger bone, but you can't judge the sex of a person standing right in front of you? Does nobody else see the irony in this?

Hodgins: Of course. But as a scientist I also see the challenge.

play a phone call between Booth and Ken Nakamura where Booth is in the diner and Nakamura is in Tokyo at a noodle stall. We dressed up 'New York Street' here to look like Tokyo and brought in a couple of rain bars and just had a torrential downpour with scooters and Japanese vehicles and stuff like that to capture that whole hustle and bustle of Tokyo. It was a lot of fun to recreate that. It's really neat to see that and think, 'Man, that really does look like he's eating at a noodle stand in Tokyo.'"

Costume designer Molly MaGinnis had great fun with this episode. "The Japanese culture is so rich for clothing and design," she says. "For the scene in a noodle shop, the director said he wanted it to look like *Blade Runner*. And he was going to have rain. We had a lot of poison greens, oranges, reds and golds, with see-through raincoats to really get that hot color against the night and the rain. We dressed all our poor extras in outlandish things and put them out there in the pouring rain. But I think we got a great look."

Bregma point: Area of the skull where the sagittal and coronal sutures joining the parietal and frontal bones come together.

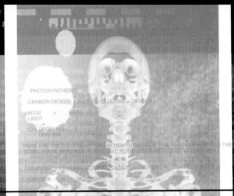

THE BEAVER IN THE OTTER

WRITTEN BY SCOTT WILLIAMS   *DIRECTED BY* BRAD TURNER

- The body of a college student is discovered in the hanging effigy of a rival team's stolen mascot suit, after dozens of students fired projectiles ranging from silverware to actual bullets at the body. Dental records identify the victim as student James Bouvier, a member of the Beta Delta Sigma fraternity.

- A "scoreboard" at the Beta Delta Sigma frat indicates that the victim had sex with one girl at the college. Bouvier had bragged that his "conquest" was Molly Briggs, a student that had previously claimed to hardly know the victim.

- The victim has twenty-three fractures, mostly from being fired on by a blunderbuss, but there are three fractures that occurred before death. The location of the injuries indicates that he tried to break a fall backwards by putting his hands out behind him, fracturing his wrist and **coccyx**.

- A small hole in the sternum indicates that something punctured the victim's **aorta**, causing him to bleed to death. The hole is consistent with a nail fired from a nail gun.

- One of the nails found in the victim shows evidence of being fired from a nail gun. It is bronze and decorative, like those on the homecoming float, which leads investigators back to Molly Briggs. She admits to firing the nail at the victim in defense when he tried to force himself on her.

GUEST STARRING: BRENDAN FEHR (JARED BOOTH), PEJ VAHDAT (ARASTOO VAZIRI), JAIMIE ALEXANDER (MOLLY BRIGGS), NICK BALLARD (GREG HARMALARD), RICK PETERS (DEAN VERNON WARNER), EDWIN HODGE (ROBERT HOOPER), MICHAEL HYATT (SHERIFF TINA MULLINS), LORNA RAVER (PROFESSOR MARLENE TWARDOSH), JONATHAN CHESNER (GARY BACON), RYAN PINKSTON (ELI ROUNDER)

In light of his new take on life, rather than let his brother get him a job, Jared Booth decides he wants to explore India on a motorcycle instead. Once Booth gets onboard with the idea, Jared suggests that he come along. Booth considers going so he can look after Jared, but decides that it's time he let Jared look after himself.

On the lighter side, Brennan's humorous reactions to the fraternity mindset seen in this episode balance out the emotional subplot and the grisly crime. While investigating the Beta Delta Sigma fraternity, Brennan thinks they've come across a group of sociopaths, but Booth tells her that it's just normal for college students to act out at that age. Not surprisingly, Brennan never acted out and begins to regret the lost opportunity. Booth helps her tap into her rebellious side by dining and dashing—though he makes sure to leave money behind first.

The college setting not only provides the theme for Brennan's internal reflections, it also serves as the setting for another interesting body. Every week the series challenges the writers to come up with a new and different way to find

Brennan: What are we looking for this time?

Booth: Love notes, photos, gray hair, orthopedic shoes; anything that provides us with the identity of Beaver's cougar.

Brennan: Beaver... otter... cougar... this case is like a day at the zoo.

their victim. This naturally means that every week also presents the production crew with a new and unique opportunity to fulfill the writers' visions.

"It's this whole thing where there is a body that's burning within a mascot suit that is suspended over a bonfire at a college pep rally," Steve Beers explains when describing the set up for the body's reveal. "All those things are mutually exclusive. Our real bodies are silicon and they'll burn, so the questions become: 'How do you control the burning mascot suit so that the body drops out of it at the

right point? How do we take what can't be burned and film it in such a way that visual effects can apply fire to the surface? And how do we do this all within the six hours we're going to have to shoot it?' Every week I get something like that, and every week I get to go through this with people like Stephen Nathan, Hart Hanson, Ian Toynton and Jan DeWitt. When we stand there and scratch our heads, I know that they're going to dig into the problems, not freak out and not point fingers. We just do what we do. It's the best job in Hollywood."

Coccyx: A small, triangular bone at the base of the spine in humans; tailbone.

Aorta: The main artery of the body, supplying blood to the circulatory system.

'Time Lapse Lifeline' by Maria Taylor, *LadyLuck*

'By and By' by Natalie Walker, *With You?*

'Save You' by Matthew Perryman Jones, *Swallow the Sea*

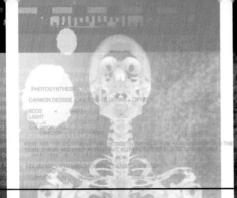

THE CRITIC IN THE CABERNET

WRITTEN BY STEPHEN NATHAN   **DIRECTED BY** KEVIN HOOKS

- Human remains are found in a wine cask at Bedford Creek vineyard.
- Grommets found with the victim that match indentations to the skull indicate that he had a craniofacial implant to secure a prosthetic hairpiece. The rare surgical procedure helps identify the victim as missing wine critic Spencer Holt.
- Scraping and gouges are present on the ribs and the sternum. Silica in the wounds matches glass found in the victim's clothes and in the wine barrel. There are five main impact points on the bone that are likely from a weapon with a circular shape. The circumference of the marks matches a wine bottle.
- Tiny fractures near the **coronal sutures** with evidence of hemorrhaging on the underside, suggest a blow to the head.
- Shards of glass found in the cask have the same thatched design as bottles from Bedford Creek, but tests prove those bottles would have smashed the skull, but not broken in the manner suggested by the wound to the sternum.
- The bottles are determined to be counterfeit, containing wine from an inferior stock. Arsenic found on the victim's clothes matches an insecticide used at the neighboring Dunwood Winery. Holt had discovered that Charles Dunwood was counterfeiting his neighbor's wine bottles, filling them with his own, cheaper product, and turning a huge profit, which is why he was killed.

GUEST STARRING: JOEL DAVID MOORE (COLIN FISHER), JEFF YAGHER (SEAN MORTENSON), CHAD WILLETT (CHARLIE DUNWOOD), LATARSHA ROSE (JENNY HOLT), SCOTTIE THOMPSON (KIM MORTENSON), DEBORAH LACEY (NURSE), SCOTT ALAN SMITH (BRUCE HANOVER), SETH MACFARLANE (VOICE OF STEWIE GRIFFEN)

During a session with Sweets, Brennan decides that she wants to have a child. Emily Deschanel sees Brennan's change of heart over having children as integral to her character's growth. "You can see how much Brennan has evolved by looking at that episode," she says. "Bones never wanted a baby before. She had no interest. And here she is soliciting Booth for his sperm. People change. I also think that when you know someone and love them, you change because of them. I think a component of why Brennan didn't want kids before was that she never loved another person enough to want a child with them; she was too scared to feel her emotions. Booth has opened her up: she's changed because of him and for him. She also wasn't emotionally available to care for a child. She still probably isn't, but she's on her way."

Booth goes to make his sperm deposit, but instead of pornography playing on the video screen, he is surprised to see Stewie from the TV series *Family Guy*. He chalks it up to the pressure of this momentous decision. When the cartoon character visits Booth again in the interrogation room, Brennan realizes something is wrong. Brennan worries that his actions, combined with hallucinations he's had earlier in the year, could be indications of

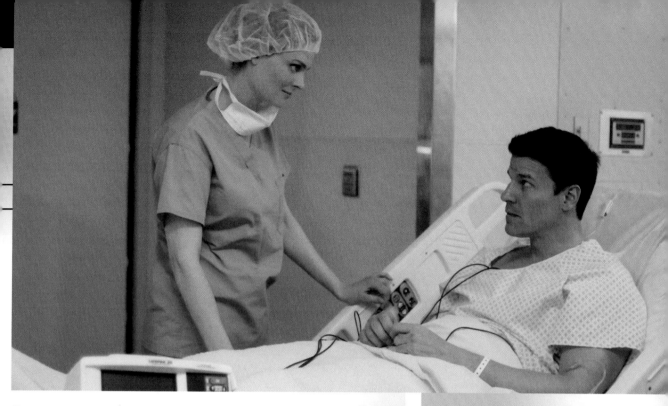

Brennan: [Booth] has traits like courage and compassion and empathy that, if they are genetically transmittable attributes—and the jury is still out on that—would be tremendous assets to my child. Sperm banks don't catalogue those traits.

Booth: Did you just say something nice?

Brennan: I gave an objective evaluation.

Booth: Oh. Because it sort of sounded nice.

something serious. She forces him to go to the hospital where it is determined that he has a brain tumor and must undergo surgery immediately.

"We've had Booth see Luc Robataille in one episode," executive producer and scribe on this episode Stephen Nathan explains, detailing the lead up to Booth's condition. "He saw a ghost when he was trapped in the boat [by the Gravedigger]. And now he's seeing Stewie when he goes to donate his sperm and also in the last interrogation scene in that episode. Brennan realizes something's wrong with Booth: he's been hallucinating. It's been very subtle. It's a situation where Booth isn't alarmed because he feels that it's normal. The other people have mentioned it in passing, but no one's really that alarmed at that point. But now, it's obviously one thing to see a ghost in a stressful situation; it's another thing to be talking to a cartoon character in an interrogation scene."

Coronal suture: A dense, fibrous connective tissue joint separating the front and parietal bones of the skull.

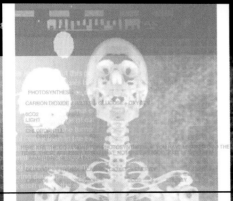

THE END IN THE BEGINNING

WRITTEN BY HART HANSON   DIRECTED BY IAN TOYNTON

SPECIAL GUEST STARS: RYAN O'NEAL (MAX KEENAN), ERIC MILLEGAN (ZACK ADDY)
GUEST STARRING: PATRICIA BELCHER (CAROLINE JULIAN), SEAN BLAKEMORE (GRAYSON BARASA), EUGENE BYRD (CARK EDISON), RYAN CARTWRIGHT (VINCENT NIGEL-MURRAY), BRENDAN FEHR (JARED BOOTH), CARLA GALLO (DAISY WICK), JOEL DAVID MOORE (COLIN FISHER), MÖTLEY CRÜE (THEMSELVES), MICHAEL GRANT TERRY (WENDELL BRAY), PEJ VAHDAT (ARASTOO VAZIRI)

The following is an outline for an original, unpublished novel by Dr. Temperance Brennan:

• A body was found at the The Lab nightclub, which is run by husband and wife Booth and Brennan. The man was shot in the chest in a bathroom stall. Blood coagulation suggests the death occurred between one and three a.m., while Brennan was still on the premises. The victim is identified as Dick Vorstenbach, a man with ties to the mafia.

• Coat check girl Daisy Wick admits to turning off the club's security cameras so she could engage in a tryst with her boyfriend, Chef Colin Fisher.

• The coroner finds fibers inside the bullet track from something used to muffle the gun that is later found among the belongings of DJ Vincent Nigel Murray.

• The hostess, Angela, admits that she innocently drew a floor plan of the club for the victim, with an X on Brennan's office.

• The bartender, Lance Sweets, finds Brennan's coat hidden in a case of gin. It had been used to muffle the gun. He and Zack burn it.

• Officer Jared Booth tells his brother that he believes Brennan was having an affair with a man trying to buy the club. The victim worked for that man and was planning to harm Brennan. Booth believes that City Councilman Max Keenan set up the whole situation in a power play spurring Jared to kill the man to protect Brennan.

Much like the kiss under the mistletoe in season three, Hart Hanson leaked the fact that Booth and Brennan would have a tryst early in the season. This meant he spent the next few months working to find a way to do it in a manner that met the audience's expectations without destroying the core relationship of his two main characters. "The fact is about a million people have asked me, 'When they get together, when they hook up in the end, is it a dream?'" Hanson says. "And I said, 'No, it's not a dream.' I'm splitting semantic hairs, and all of them are going to get mad at me. I'll say, 'No, it was a combination of a hallucination and a book.'"

The story of Brennan's latest book follows characters based on her and Booth along with the people in their lives. "It's an alternate reality," Hanson explains. "The nightclub looks exactly like the lab. Everyone in the show is from the show. Everyone you've seen before. Everyone has the same name, but they're playing a slightly different version of themselves. It's a completely and utterly different show, except everything in it is familiar. And there's a murder in their nightclub. It involves all our regulars, everybody. All the interns are there. Zack is there. None of them have the same jobs, none of them are exactly the same person. The idea is to

Voiceover: You see two people and you think, "They belong together. They love one another." But nothing happens. Perhaps it's because, for some people, the thought of losing so much control over personal happiness is unbearable. If something, anything happened to that other person, it would be death. If they left you, it would be death... Yet, the truth is, some burdens are not burdens at all. Like wings, they have weight, we feel that weight on our backs, but they are a burden that lifts us. Burdens that allow us to fly.

write them as a bit more of their inner character. So they all have a role that is their inner character."

The fact that Booth and Brennan get together in a fiction may not satisfy all the fans, and, just to make it all the more complicated, Booth wakes up from the coma unsure if its the real Brennan with him or the dream version.

"People are dying for them to be together," Hanson says. "The reason people are dying for them to be together is because we've created that need. If we

fulfilled it, put them together, everyone would be happy for about two minutes and then they would be bored with our series. I keep saying: 'If I'm going to remove the unresolved romantic tension between them it has to be replaced by something else.' Everyone always has suggestions and none of them are as powerful as a nascent love affair, of a love affair that has not been consummated. That's a real powerful engine from the earliest times. From Adam and Eve. You mess with it with great trepidation."

'**Now You Know**' by The Classic
'**Ridin**' by Miss Eighty 6
'**Don't Know What I Want**' by Random Impulse, *Full Metal Alchemist*
'**Push That Thing 08 (Sharooz Remix)**' by Dave Aude/DJ Dan, *2 Audacious*
'**Let's Get it Crackin**' by Deetown Allstars, *Deetown Presents: Music from Chicks Shows*
'**Neverending Summer**' by Dayplayer
'**Caveman**' by Dayplayer?
'**Dirty Dancin**' by The DNC, *The DNC*

SPECIAL AGENT SEELEY BOOTH

On the surface, Special Agent Seeley Booth seems like a pretty straightforward kind of guy. In a world populated with genius I.Q.s, and rife with personality quirks, he's the street smart F.B.I. agent who leads with his gut and an incredible amount of heart. Yet, beneath that knight-in-shining-armor exterior lies a troubled past that he is only now allowing others to see.

When the series opened, considering that the world of *Bones* was largely filled with the Jeffersonian staff, Booth was very much the outsider. He worked very closely with all of these people, but, with the exception of Brennan, kept each one at arm's length. Over the years, there has been a lessening of that distance as they have become a close-knit team that even has the new interns quick to proclaim that they proudly work for Booth, as seen in 'Fire in the Ice.'

Booth is a deeply religious, military man with some fairly liberal views. That dichotomy makes for an interesting dynamic between him and Brennan's more straightforward worldview, and that dynamic is the core of the series. Their debates on everything from religion and society to sex and love are the key to their relationship. Though, at first glance, it might appear that it is Booth who is having the greater effect on Brennan when it comes to evolving as a character, there is no doubt that his proximity to her has helped him grow as well.

Their kiss under the mistletoe in 'The Santa in the Slush' was a key moment in the Booth/Brennan relationship, and that episode as a whole said probably more about Booth's feelings toward Brennan than any other. Brennan was forced into the kiss to provide a happy holiday for her family. It was an uncharacteristically emotional gift for her to give, but she did have motivation for the kiss beyond simply locking lips with Booth. Booth, on the other hand, had nothing at stake: he was merely helping out his friend. At least, that's how it could easily be explained away instead of

"I WILL BE THE GUY IN THE 'COCKY' BELT BUCKLE AND THE SNAZZY RENTED TUX."

bringing his complicated emotions into the equation. At the end of the episode, however, there was a moment that was almost more touching than the kiss. Booth and his son, Parker, set up a Christmas tree outside the prison so that Brennan's family would not miss out on a traditional holiday. It was a gesture that the normally unsentimental Brennan would fully appreciate.

The first two seasons of the show focused more on Booth's military history and how his past career as a sniper affects him to this day. But that element of his past was never more deeply explored than in the fourth season with 'The Hero in the Hold.' In an episode where the Squints had to rescue Booth, the audience learned more about his hidden pain when he interacted with the ghost of a man who had died under his command; the man he named his son after.

The fact that Seeley Booth is a father is never far from the writers' minds when they are developing his character. Aside from the many episodes that Parker has been seen in, there are numerous examples from the series in which Booth's fatherhood comes into play on a case or in a conversation. Unlike some shows that trot out a child actor for special episodes, Booth is a father, first and foremost, and this fact is intrinsic to the development of his character into the fourth season.

While the series explored Booth's military history more in the early years, the later seasons have delved more deeply into his family, revealing secrets that he'd previously held close to the vest. Through his work with Dr. Gordon Wyatt, the audience learned that Booth had some darkness in his childhood, which he would explore further with Dr. Sweets in seasons three and, more notably, four. The son of an abusive alcoholic, Booth told Brennan and Sweets that if it weren't for his grandfather, he would have taken his life as a teen. He also admitted to serving as the *de facto* father to his younger brother, Jared, who was introduced to the audience in 'The Con Man in the Meth Lab.' As Brennan's family drama wound down, it seemed as though Booth's heated up.

David Boreanaz and Emily Deschanel share a joke on location while filming 'Yanks in the U.K.'

The audience was initially concerned by what it meant for Booth and Brennan when Camille Saroyan, a former love, came back into his life in the second season, but their romantic tension was dismissed fairly quickly. In its place developed one of the stronger friendships in the series. Booth got to be there for Cam at her father's birthday party when she hasn't told her family that they were no longer dating. In return, she was immediately at his door when Brennan announced that she had solicited his sperm in her attempt to have a child.

The decision for Brennan to have a child came up rather quickly in a therapy session with Sweets. Although she assured Booth that she expected no more involvement in the child's life after his donation, it was that same assurance that ultimately convinced him to decline. It was also one of the surest signs of his deeper emotional attachment to Brennan. Much the way either Angela or Hodgins could have simply said the right word to keep their relationship together,

the writers felt that Booth or Brennan could have been on the verge of making a commitment that was stronger than some donated DNA. Booth's decision came in the heat of the moment as Brennan realized something was medically wrong with him, but that was not the reason for his declining to help.

"He makes the decision not to give her the sperm for reasons of the heart," Hart Hanson explains. "If only one of them had said, 'Listen, I'm not going to do this like a science experiment. Why don't we try and make this work? Why don't we have a child together in the usual way?' Booth realizes if they're not going to do it that way, then he's not going to do it and she's not going to want the baby without him. Which is very romantic in an odd way. When he says 'no', she says, 'I'm not interested anymore.' Which I think most of our audience will realize means that she's nuts about him." That key moment in their relationship will certainly play out in future seasons, once Booth recovers from his coma.

DR. TEMPERANCE BRENNAN

Dr. Temperance Brennan is based on an amalgam of characters that have evolved into a unique individual. The name comes from the character in the bestselling book series written by noted author Kathy Reichs. The world she inhabits is a combination of that character and Reichs herself, blending fact with fiction and the creator with her creation. But the television series creator, Hart Hanson, didn't stop with Reichs and the literary

Brennan when he developed his version of Temperance. Hanson created a new personality with the intelligently empirical forensic anthropologist and, over four seasons, Emily Deschanel has given that character life.

Bones, as a series, opened with Brennan and Booth negotiating their relatively new partnership where she offers her expertise as a forensic anthropologist in some of the most gruesome F.B.I. cases to come across the agent's desk. As she would remind Booth in the fourth season episode 'The Passenger in the Oven' it was Brennan's insistence that she accompany him in the field that laid the foundation for their working relationship. The personal bond simmering beneath the surface was clear to everyone from the start—except the two characters themselves.

Under the employ of the Jeffersonian Institute, Brennan oversees a team of scientists that Booth refers to as the "Squints," where she initially toiled under the fatherly eye of the man who hired her, Dr. Daniel Goodman. In the second season, she started reporting to the newly announced head of forensics, Dr. Camille Saroyan. At first, the pair clashed over their different work styles, but they have learned to work together as a team to solve each case, though they do butt heads from time to time in a good natured manner.

On a personal level, Temperance Brennan's backstory is far more complicated than her work life. Brennan's parents abandoned her and her brother Russ when she was fifteen.

"MY BRAIN IS FAR MORE VALUABLE TO SOCIETY THAN MY UTERUS."

Considering that Russ was only a few years older than her and unable to fill in for their parents, he left her in foster care. In the first two seasons of the series, Brennan reunited with her brother and father when she learned that her childhood was even more confused than she had thought: her parents had been fugitives and her very identity was unknown to her. She was born Joy Keenan, but her name was changed when her family went into hiding.

Many personal trials would affect Brennan over the third and fourth seasons of the show where the personal continued to mix with the professional. The groundwork had already been laid for her complicated family dynamic, and things certainly did not get easier for her when Booth captured her father, Max Keenan. He was arrested for killing an F.B.I. deputy director in order to protect his children. During the third season Brennan's brother returned and her father was placed on trial. Having her family back in her life certainly affected Brennan. What was once a black-and-white world in which her father was a bad guy became shades of gray as Brennan learned to accept that sometimes people have good reasons for doing bad things.

While Brennan's family situation played out, the writers also had the chance to move her and Booth's relationship forward without actually bringing them together. 'The Santa in the Slush' had the notable moment where the pair shared their first kiss. The moment may have come out of blackmail when Caroline Julian made it a requirement for her to agree to help Brennan's family spend the holiday together in jail, but Emily Deschanel notes that, no matter the motivation, the kiss was still a kiss. "Before that moment, both of them could deny their attraction for the other," she explains. "That kiss was a turning point. After that experience, neither of them could deny their feelings for the other, at least to themselves."

The family storyline also helped serve as a launching point to bring a new character into Brennan's life. Dr. Sweets was introduced as the F.B.I. psychologist charged with determining if the Booth/Brennan partnership should continue in the light of Booth arresting her father. Though Brennan gives little credence to the "soft science" of psychology, the sessions with Sweets help give her a greater insight into herself and Booth, which is why she agreed to let them continue past the point where they were required in 'The Verdict in the Story.' It was a good decision as two episodes later Brennan's entire world would be rocked. 'The Pain in the Heart' was a notable episode for the series as a whole and for the character of Brennan. It was the moment where the audience, and she, learned that her trusted assistant, Dr. Zack Addy, was working with the serial killer the team is hunting. Emily Deschanel believes that Brennan blames herself for the situation that shook her character to the core. "I think Brennan was very upset that she didn't notice any signs," the actress notes. "She doubted her ability to judge someone's character. It's pretty upsetting when someone you trust does

Emily Deschanel has her makeup touched up in view of the Houses of Parliament, while on location for 'Yanks in the U.K.'

something horrible. You blame yourself. But she's working through it."

As Brennan moved through the fourth season, more than any season prior, she began to question her worldview as she increasingly saw Booth as an example of a person she would like to resemble. Her interactions with Sweets and his "soft science" became more prevalent as she consulted the doctor on how to live more emotionally and react to the emotions of others, as seen in the episode 'The Bones that Foam.' It seems she has begun to take to heart the criticism she has suffered through the years for her inability to connect with people, which was likely one of the elements leading to her abrupt decision at the end of the season to have a child.

"To put it simply, I think Brennan has become much more fun over the last few seasons," Emily Deschanel says of her character's evolution. "Her walls have come down. In the beginning, she was uptight: she controlled her emotions and her life. Brennan was scared to open up because of being hurt in the past. She also was incredibly socially awkward. I guess Brennan is still pretty socially awkward and in-sensitive. But she's aware of it, and she's making an effort to change."

ANGELA MONTENEGRO

"I think that she's a pretty complicated character," Michaela Conlin says when discussing the many moods of her character, forensic artist Angela Montenegro. "I think that her exterior of wanting to have fun and get a drink and 'C'est la vie,' that she shows to the world is in a lot of contrast to who she actually is. She's a very private person. I won't go so far as saying confused, but I think she's in the middle of trying to figure a lot of things out. But she doesn't want other people to know that. I think that's a really great thing to play."

From the start, Angela functioned on a number of levels. The devil-may-care free spirit appears to be clearly in

conflict with the sterile world of the lab that surrounds her. "She's incredibly empathetic," Conlin says. "She really is the heart of that lab, though I do also think she has to figure her own heart out, too." No more was this in evidence than when Angela was the one Squint who refused to testify against her best friend's father in 'The Verdict in the Story.'

Early on in the series Angela told Brennan that she'd worked at the Jeffersonian longer than her usual gigs, and yet there she remains. The gruesome crimes still get to her, though she is not as deeply affected by them as she used to be, at least on the surface. It is clear that she still loves Jack Hodgins, but she cannot be with him. The audience often questions her actions, but that may be largely due to her own personality just naturally being at odds with itself. "Hart Hanson writes these highly functioning women that have some faults," Conlin says. "Every woman I know is like that."

Angela's faults seem to have been at war with her heart lately. Through the first two seasons, she and Hodgins had a simmering attraction not unlike the one between Booth and Brennan. The big difference was that the couple gave in to their emotions and allowed themselves the workplace romance. However, the cracks began to show when Angela made Hodgins redo his marriage proposal until he got it right. Even then, the walk down the aisle was halted when Angela's carefree past caught up with her and she was reminded that she was already married.

"THIS IS ONE OF THOSE TIMES I KNOW WHAT'S RIGHT AND EVERYBODY ELSE IS JUST CONFUSED."

Still, she tried to make things work even though it apparently went against her nature. Michaela Conlin maintains that none of it was intentional on her character's part. "It has been complicated," she admits. "Angela really wanted to have a conventional wedding and a conventional relationship, and get married and wear a dress. I think that she sort of forgot along that road about how unconventional she is. She really tried to make it work. They hired the investigators. She got hypnotized. Somewhere along the line I think she had a feeling that she wants to be free."

Angela and Hodgins broke up during 'Yanks in the U.K. Part 2,' even though the first part of that episode made it clear to the audience that they were meant to be together. The producers have stated that they still believe that the pair is meant to be, but that's not to say there won't be challenges and personal revelations that get in the way.

Season four saw a tremendous amount of change to Angela's character as she examined her approach to the world. She briefly rekindled her relationship with her former love, Roxie Lyons, but that, too, ended when Roxie recognized that, in spite of all that Angela had been through, she hadn't really changed. "She's really trying to figure out who she is," Conlin reiterates. "I think that the first season was her telling everyone who she was. It was sort of her controlling what it was. I think now you're getting to see other people coming up from her past and her family. And I think people are starting to really figure out where she is."

The end of her relationship with Roxie, followed quickly by a brief, noncommittal tumble with Hodgins, sent Angela to Brennan for advice in 'The Salt in the Wounds.' When Brennan agreed with Angela's approach to her love life, Angela realized she was in trouble and sought out further advice from Sweets. The young doctor proposed that maybe it was time for her to remove sex from the equation in her relationships, to see if she could connect on another level. "The celibacy storyline has actually been a real blast to play," Conlin says. "It was a brilliant idea to put a cork in the bottle of a very shaken soda. She's single and wanting to kind of screw everything that's not nailed down, so to speak. For some reason she takes the advice of this young shrink, because she knows she needs guidance from somebody. She begrudgingly listens to this twenty-three year old shrink and thinks it might do something to aid her relationships. It's been really fun to play because when you're not allowed to do something or talk about something, it's sort of all you want to do. It's like the pink elephant in the room. It's been really fun to hit on young, innocent interns and fellow cast members. Angela will hit on pretty much everyone—even the skeleton on the table at this point!"

The blending of comedy with the serious emotional issues is something that the writers of *Bones* strive for in their approach to the show. It is a balance that is difficult to maintain, but allows the actors to explore those various levels to their characters and get into outrageous and emotional situations. Angela and Hodgins sought closure several times throughout the fourth season, but a moment in 'The End in the Beginning' certainly reinforced the idea that Hodgela is not over yet.

DR. JACK HODGINS

"When we first met Jack he was a hot head, just all anger," actor TJ Thyne notes of his character. "They loved the idea of him being in anger management and that everything seemed to... well... annoy him. I believe when a show begins you need those broad colors to separate one character from the next: Oh she's the pretty one, he's the nerdy one, she's the down-to-earth-one, he's the angry one... It just helps establish immediate, identifiable character traits for the audience to associate with. As the show went on through season one and definitely through season two, we got to see all the other sides of

Jack, his full spectrum of colors, and that's where I think he is most different today than day one of season one. Jack is not just a loud, angry scientist, he's a flesh and blood guy with big fears, and deep loves."

Dr. Jack Hodgins is a more fully realized character by the end of season four, with dozens of storylines under his belt that added to his history and allowed him to grow. In the early seasons, Hodgins was known primarily for the wild conspiracy theories he wove. Occasionally, he would hit close to the mark in the real world, but generally speaking no one took him too seriously, least of all the actor who played him. "I love playing every aspect of Jack, I really do," Thyne says. "I feel very lucky as an actor to have a character I enjoy playing so much. As for the conspiracy theory side of Jack, sure it's fun. Look at the fascination we as a society have with conspiracies. Look at the success of novels and films like *Angels & Demons* and shows like the one our own some-time-director David Duchovny was on for years, *The X-Files*. It's a lot of fun to play."

But the fun turned serious in the third season when Hodgins' theories proved all too real. The Gormogon serial killer storyline was effectively launched off Hodgins' knowledge of the arcane, as it related to the history of secret societies. From there, the writers built a twisted individual who—had the season gone the way they'd hoped—would have tapped into Hodgins' darker side and cast a real doubt on his character. Unfortunately, the strike-shortened season did not allow for a full exploration of the Gormogon, though it

"KING OF THE LAB!"

did touch upon Hodgins as a possible suspect, before Zack was revealed in a decision by the writers that Thyne admits, "Killed me. And killed Jack. It was so hard to take."

Hodgins fell into a depression in the early episodes of season four that grew partly from his difficulty accepting the fact that his best friend worked with a killer and partly due to his breakup with Angela. He was snapping at everyone, blaming near strangers for problems in his life from years earlier. He even stopped doing his beloved experiments because they reminded him too much of Zack.

Eventually, in 'The Finger in the Nest' Hodgins sought help from Sweets, who told him that his reaction was purely natural. Sweets pointed out that the mere fact that Hodgins continued at the Jeffersonian Institution, when he was more than rich enough to never put in another day of work in his life, indicated that the entomologist had not given up on living, which was a very good sign. Hodgins had, however, given up on his relationship with Angela. In a moment that confused some fans, and maybe even the characters themselves, Hodgela ended their relationship. But it was a moment that TJ Thyne kind of understood. "She stirs the air he breathes," the romantic actor says, describing Hodgins' feelings toward Angela. "But while she's running in and out of relationships with others, and kissing others, and wanting to sleep with others, it's just too hard to keep taking. So, he has finally accepted letting her go.

If she, on her own, finds her way back to him, he'll drop to his knees and raise his hands high to heaven with a mighty cry of '*Thank you!*'(Which we've actually seen him do in a more subtle form throughout the last few years.) But in the interim, in the meanwhile, he moves on, and hopes. Which is what that moment toward the end of season four with her earring is all about.

"He's had to tell her that as much as he *loves* meeting up in the storage room, it can't just be that for him. He wants more. He wants all of her so he can continue to give her all of him and oh so very much more. What do I hope? That they make it. What do I think? Well... you'll have to wait and see."

Though Jack Hodgins—and TJ Thyne—may be pining for Angela, the character has started to move on. 'The Cinderella in the Cardboard' was a major milestone in Hodgins accepting his life as a single man and meeting a group of new friends with the help of one of the interns. His conspiracy theories were starting to come out once again and his weird and wonderful experiments resumed with the cast of rotating interns that he was able to have fun with. It seems he's gotten a bit of the old Jack back, while still embracing the new facets of his personality.

"Season four, we know this guy," Thyne says. "'Oh him, that's Jack.' The audience knows how Jack will react to every circumstance before he's even put into it. They know what will make him laugh, they know what he most loves in life, they know where and why he hides his vulnerability and that means you really know someone. Jack Hodgins, season four, is the guy you've come to rely on who will always help you find that answer with a whole hell of a lot of sarcasm attached. And he's the guy you silently root for. You hope he gets the girl and ends up happy... Or, maybe that's just me."

DR. CAMILLE SAROYAN

D r. Camille Saroyan was introduced in the second season of *Bones* and slowly worked her way into the audience's hearts. There was initial concern from the fans who were afraid that she had come in only to provide an obstacle for the Booth and Brennan relationship. And certainly, there was some rekindling of the affair between her and Booth, but they quickly realized they worked better as friends as the writers worked her into the dynamic of the Jeffersonian. Since then she has bonded with the diverse personalities on the staff and made a place for herself on the team.

"I think certainly all of the relationships have deepened," says Tamara Taylor, describing how Cam has grown with the show. "When she came on the scene in the second season she was not only reestablishing her relationship with Booth, she was clearly establishing her position within the Jeffersonian and making sure that it was understood that she was the authority figure there. I think because that relationship is so clearly defined now, what has started to happen is she can just enjoy everybody. Everybody knows that Cam is the boss; everybody knows that she's the final word. So now she can loosen up and just appreciate and have a good time."

Booth is Cam's closest friend on the show. She knows his history, is friends with his brother, and has even allowed her own family to think she is still dating the man. They have both had the opportunity to be there for each other over the seasons, when cases hit too close to home or parts of their personal lives blended into their work.

As the head of the forensics division of the Medico-Legal lab, Cam is, technically, Dr. Brennan's boss. However, Brennan's credentials also place her in a powerful position in the lab. This led to some initial friction between the characters, especially considering they both approach the work of examining remains in very different ways. To this day, they may butt heads once in a while as each exerts her position, but it is done

"I'M A WISECRACKING PATHOLOGIST WITH A DARK SENSE OF HUMOR."

with more of a sense of camaraderie, since Cam has also proven that she is an expert in her field, and has therefore won Brennan's respect.

As the chief among the Squints, it's no surprise that Cam is largely confined to the lab, overseeing the work of Angela, Hodgins, Zack and the rotating staff of interns in the fourth season. Since much of the work that Booth and Brennan do in the field consists of gruesome murders and dramatic investigations, much of the comedy of the series is left to the denizens of the lab. Tamara Taylor is a particular fan of the comedic scenes that the writers give her in almost every script. "It's so much fun," she says about playing the comedy. "The writers are so amazing for this show. They write great, funny stuff. Then, getting on to the set

and playing with everybody and trying to find more, trying to mine for the funnies, it's one of my favorite things."

Often Cam does find herself as the straight person to the comedic foibles of the Squints, but she is definitely quick with a quip and, on occasion, gets some egg on her face as well. One particularly awkward situation arose in 'Yanks in the U.K.' when a kindly offer to give Angela's ex-husband a ride to the airport ended up with them in bed. "It seems like Cam is very rarely caught with her pants down or caught unawares," Taylor says. "I think she was a little unbuttoned in that episode, which was really, really fun."

Cam is often the adult in the lab, forced to be the one to come running whenever there is a biohazard lockdown. She chastised Hodgins and Zack many times in season three for their unorthodox experiments that had a tendency to go wrong. This led to a closer friendship with her "Zacaroni" considering that, in a six-person regular cast, Booth and Brennan were paired up and Hodgins and Angela were linked romantically. This growing bond eventually led to the heartbreaking moment in 'The Pain in the Heart' where Cam was sitting in the hospital with Zack when Booth and Brennan arrived to reveal that Zack was working with Gormogon. And it led to her tearful admission in the final scene, "I knew the first day I met Zack he'd cause me pain."

Following Zack's departure, Cam took on the responsibility of encouraging Dr. Brennan's interns, since the forensic anthropologist is not as adept at social interaction. Though Tamara Taylor freely admits to missing Eric Millegan deeply, this recurring cast of semi-regulars has opened up the show for her in new ways. "It's nice that there's something new every week," Taylor says. "There's a different joke, a different kind of comedy. There's a different storyline every week that sort of keeps it interesting."

But nothing was more interesting to the actress than when she read the script that informed her she was about to become a mother. To a teenage girl. 'The Doctor in the Den' could be considered Cam's "spotlight episode" in the fourth season. It introduced the audience—and the actress—to an important period in Cam's past when she was engaged to a man that she lived with for two years. She ultimately called off the wedding because he could not be faithful. The decision had been difficult, and even more so because it meant that she also left behind his daughter, whom she had grown to love as if the girl was her own.

Years later, the teenage girl comes back into Cam's life following her father's murder. It may not be the most obvious choice for Cam, but she's making do the best she can. "She's certainly not Mother Nature," Tamara Taylor admits. "I don't know if she's taking to it as naturally as possibly other women would. She's more like Miranda in *Sex and the City*. Definitely not an intuitive mom, but she loves the experience. She's a bit of a stumble-bum, but she's having a good time."

DR. LANCE SWEETS

r. Lance Sweets joined *Bones* at the start of the third season, following in the footsteps of Booth's previous F.B.I.-ordered therapist, Dr. Gordon Wyatt. The differences between the two therapists couldn't have been more pronounced. Dr. Wyatt was a large, jovially intimidating man who held sway over Booth while meeting after the agent discharged his weapon on a defenseless clown head on an ice cream truck. The relationship borne out of that pairing inspired the writers to come up with new story ideas to integrate Dr. Wyatt into the show as a profiler for the F.B.I. Stephen Fry, the actor playing Wyatt, had too busy a schedule to commit to such a role, but the writers were so enamored by the idea of what a psychologist could bring to the cases that Dr. Lance Sweets was born.

"It grew from just an F.B.I.-appointed visit, to him basically trying to get them to open up to each other," John Francis Daley says, describing how his character, Sweets, came into the show and into the Booth and Brennan relationship. "I think he noticed that the chemistry between them was pretty strong. And now that Sweets has been brought in to help with the cases and profiling and helping them find the murderers, I think they actually look to him as a somewhat valuable resource. Before, I don't think anyone took him seriously. They would never admit to him that they think he's valuable, but I think secretly they think that he's helpful to them."

That help began when Booth and Brennan were assigned to meet with Sweets after Booth arrested Brennan's father, as Booth's superiors were concerned that this would put a strain on their partnership. Under that directive, Sweets met with the pair regularly throughout the third season up to the trial of Max Keenan. During that time, he poked and prodded at the relationship, clearly sensing the underlying romantic tension that Booth and Brennan either pointedly ignored or could not see at all. It was not an arrangement that either of his subjects were originally comfortable with, which often led to him butting heads with them.

"Brennan thinks of Sweets as a pseudo-scientist," Daley explains. "Whereas Sweets thinks that Brennan's hard science doesn't really live up to the complexities of the mind

"SOMETIMES I HATE HARD SCIENCE. I KNOW THAT MIGHT SEEM IMMATURE, BUT THAT'S HOW I FEEL."

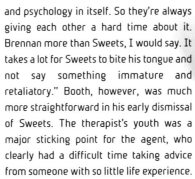

and psychology in itself. So they're always giving each other a hard time about it. Brennan more than Sweets, I would say. It takes a lot for Sweets to bite his tongue and not say something immature and retaliatory." Booth, however, was much more straightforward in his early dismissal of Sweets. The therapist's youth was a major sticking point for the agent, who clearly had a difficult time taking advice from someone with so little life experience.

As season three progressed, Booth and Brennan became so accustomed to his presence in their lives that they agreed to continue to see him even after Max's trial had come to a close. Sweets offered profiling services for their cases in exchange for additional sessions in which he could use the pair as subjects for a book he was going to write on their partnership.

Sweets' involvement in the crimes also meant that he would spend more time with the Squints and develop relationships in the series outside of Booth and Brennan. Numerous times throughout the fourth season, various members of the team would consult with him on their troubles. It once bothered him how they would just drop by unannounced, until Cam pointed out that he should take it as a compliment.

Unlike the other characters, Sweets seems able to have stable relationships. When he first entered their lives, he was romantically linked to an older woman. Their relationship was going along fine, until he added a night out with Booth and Brennan into the mix. Suddenly his girlfriend saw the problems they had and ended it with him, which cleared the way for a new romance in season four.

Dr. Brennan's inability to find a replacement for Zack worked in Sweets' favor when one of her interns turned out to be the comely Daisy Wick. They began to see each other clandestinely but, once Brennan decided to fire her, their relationship went public and they could be annoyingly cute together in front of his coworkers.

But all is not lightness and love in Lance Sweets' world. In 'Double Trouble in the Panhandle,' the audience learned that Sweets had been adopted. But it was 'Mayhem on a Cross' that revealed just how difficult his life pre-adoption had been. When Brennan ripped off his shirt to staunch the blood on a knife victim, she saw scars across his back that were the result of childhood abuse by his natural parents. His adoptive parents both died shortly before Sweets met Booth and Brennan and it would seem that he has imprinted on them, like a baby duck, and looks to them for the family he is missing.

"Sweets probably doesn't have a lot of close friends because of the circumstances of him graduating through his school so quickly and probably getting a lot of slack from the people that he's working with who are all older than him," Daley says. "I think he absolutely does appreciate the fact that Booth and Brennan have taken him under their wing and allowed him to join the group. It's a kind of vulnerable side I don't think Sweets is comfortable showing, because he does think of himself as probably the most brilliant person there, aside from, maybe, Brennan. So it takes a little while for him to open up to them in terms of his past and his former experiences."

That may be true of his character, but two seasons in, Daley is fully absorbed into the group behind the scenes, and he's enjoying every minute of it. "In terms of the work," Daley says, "when we're all together—the Squints and Brennan and Booth are together in a scene—it's always the most fun for me, because everyone at one point cracks up and makes it difficult and at the same time really fun to work. Everyone has a sense of humor. You forget that you're actually working and not just goofing around. That definitely shows the natural chemistry between all the characters."

DR. ZACK ADDY

Adorably awkward Dr. Zack Addy, as played by Eric Millegan, is logical to a considerable fault. Though the actor who played him was among the older members of the cast, Zack was the youngest character in the team, both in age and in spirit. In a way, this made him seem like the innocent "kid brother" to the other characters. He was Hodgins' best friend and cohort in crazy experiments. Angela looked after him; Cam became a close friend. Brennan was likely the one who most understood him, while Booth provided guidance for one of the toughest decisions Zack likely ever made.

This decision occurred at the end of the second season. While his friends were preparing for the wedding of Angela and Hodgins, Zack was getting ready to go to war. "Some people misunderstood why he was in Iraq," Eric Millegan notes, clearing up the confusion. "Some people think that he was there actually serving in the military. What he was actually doing was identifying remains. It's what he does. He's very good at that."

Working with the dead may have been his particular skill, but it was the living that caused him problems. Citing a failure to integrate with the unit he was assigned to, Zack was asked to leave. Though his friends were certainly thrilled to have him home, the rejection fell hard on the character. Eric Millegan regrets that they could not explore the storyline further, but understands that it was out of the writers' control. He explains, "I was told we were going to learn more about what happened to him in Iraq, but the strike kind of derailed that plan."

The writers' strike also affected the end of Zack's season, and what became the end of his time as a regular character on the show. The Gormogon story had always been intended to end with a revelation that rocked the world of the Jeffersonian staff. Early on, the writers had intended to kill off Zack. But a change of heart led to him becoming the Gormogon's apprentice instead. "When we came back from the strike, we shot the court episode and the one where we find out Zack works with Gormogon," Millegan explains. "They were both very fun episodes acting wise for me. Even though I found out I was not going to be on the show on a regular basis, I came back to have two great episodes to work on. Doing those bed scenes in the hospital was just great fun. Even though Zack's tortured and upset, playing tortured and upset is great. It's very fun.

"I want to thank the fans for connecting with the character," Millegan says in conclusion. "I read everything on the internet that people were saying before and after that last episode. People were upset, and it felt great to know that my character connected to the audience. I was in Germany when the episode aired where you find out I'm not the killer. I went on the internet and I read the message board as the episode went on. I couldn't wait to see what they thought when they found out I wasn't the killer. They were all excited. The fans, I thank you so much for loving the character and appreciating the work I do and appreciating the writing of the show, which I think has upset them and then made people happy, as well."

"YOU ARE CORRECT, THERE'S AN INCONSISTENCY IN MY REASONING."

THE INTERNS

One of the repercussions of Zack being institutionalized for assisting the Gormogon killer was that the show needed to fill the void left by the character. While everyone agrees that Zack is irreplaceable, the more literal fact of Brennan needing an assistant to do the lab work while she is in the field cannot be ignored. But the writers knew that anyone they brought in so soon after Zack's departure was going to be difficult for the audience to accept.

"One of the things I wanted to avoid was what poor Tamara had to go through when she came in as Cam," Hart Hanson reveals. "Which was the audience turned on her. She was a new member, and it took a while for her to be accepted. Now she's very popular as near as we can tell,

as testing and the message boards say. But it was a rough go for an actress who came in and did a very good job and was just excoriated on the message boards. I said, 'Don't look at them. Do not look at the message boards. We like what you're doing and so will they.' But what we didn't want was to go through that again so soon."

The producers knew that if they just replaced a character that was not only popular with the audience, but with the cast and the crew as well, it would be a difficult fit. "He was Hodgins' best friend," Hanson notes. "Brennan felt very close to him. He freaked Booth out, but Booth had a grudging respect for his brain. Cam had become very fond of him. To pop someone into that slot felt wrong."

The producers' instincts about replacing Zack were reinforced when they began auditioning possible actors to fill the void, beginning with Ryan Cartwright, who ultimately went on to play the English intern, Vincent Nigel-Murray. "He came in and did this incredibly good audition," Hanson reveals. "He was very funny. But when you look at him you go, 'Tall, thin, young, baby-faced, pale, floppy-hared: we've been here before.' To throw him into that slot would have been crazy. Between the question, 'Well, how do we use him?' and 'What do we do to replace Zack?' The rotating idea came up. To be honest, I thought we'd do four or six and then pick somebody. But it has so opened up the stories in the lab. It has so given us more life in the lab. Each one of them has been quite popular so we decided to keep doing that for a while. We just kept rotating actors in and out of that, depending on the story, because it's been worth it for us. It brings some life into the lab. It increases the size of the ensemble without increasing the size of the ensemble."

The actors agree that the recurring cast members have added to the dynamic in the lab scenes. TJ Thyne, in particular, is enthusiastic about them. "We love our interns!" he gushes. "The actors playing these roles are a blast to have on set! We feel like our family grew a little when they began to show up, especially for those of us in the lab. Since Brennan is, for the most part, off with Booth these days, having a new intern week to week is a blast for me and Tamara because we've made all these new friends who each bring a unique spin and energy to the lab and to how we act as actors."

At the start of 'The Girl in the Mask' Brennan consults with Booth over which of the interns would finally fill Zack's place. Their conversation is interrupted when a mystery comes calling, but Brennan does know that it is finally time to move on. Though the question is not resolved by season's end, the actors had one last shot to leave their mark on the audience in an alternate reality that saw the return of most of the interns in slightly different roles.

Dr. Clark Edison (Eugene Byrd): The one option already in possession of a doctorate, Dr. Clark Edison had initially been brought in to replace Zack when he left for Iraq. He later helped defend Brennan's father in his murder trial when the Squints were called for the prosecutor. Considered the most astute and experienced of the candidates, Clark himself had trouble fitting into a workplace that is much more lax than he would like.

Daisy Wick (Carla Gallo): Daisy was the first intern to be dismissed when her overeager attitude did not compensate for the lack of skills required to work for Brennan. She may not have become a member of the team, but she managed to get a relationship out of the deal, meeting and falling for Dr. Sweets and sticking around after she wore out her welcome at the lab.

Scott Starret (Michael Badalucco): The oldest of the interns, Starret was a man of many, many hats. Preferring to live his life collecting experiences, he moved on from the Jeffersonian to a new position after a brief visit.

Wendell Bray (Michael Grant Terry): Wendell seems to be the most normal of the choices, and the one that Booth most connected to. He grew up on the streets and had a number of people in his life that he feels indebted to for getting him where he is today.

Colin Fisher (Joel David Moore): Perfectly at home surrounded by death, Fisher is the most morbid of the interns. His constant pronouncements on the pointlessness of it all certainly do nothing to liven up the morgue.

Vincent Nigel-Murray (Ryan Cartwright): Mr. Nigel Murray is another one who fits well with the staff despite his quirk of spouting off random facts that have nothing to do with the case. It may be his way of helping him focus, but it was distracting to the team as they worked to gather the evidence.

Arastoo Vaziri (Pej Vahdat): Vaziri's tendency to speak in onomatopoeia was a particularly notable personality quirk. The Muslim intern's routine prayer breaks did disrupt the process, particularly for Hodgins who is pretty much opposed to all forms of religion.